This book is distinguished in two ways—

1. It focuses on the years *before* retirement— **the pre-retirement period**, in contrast with most books about retirement.

The authors suggest how to shape what may seem like "the last chapter" of our working life into "the first chapter" of our new identity and a satisfying life after retirement.

2. Instead of focusing primarily on finances, *55 and Counting: A Guide to Pre-Retirement* examines **all** aspects of our lives—changing identity, expanding friendships, valuing time, connecting our past to our future, developing a network of care, being mindful of health, starting to think about future housing preferences, and planning a smooth transition—all in addition to financial planning.

Making purposeful decisions and changes in the years before we "turn in our keys" can lead to much less stressful and more fulfilling retirement years.

The authors capture the multiple factors of this major moment in our lives with honesty and grace.

For more information about this book and other titles published by Walnut Street Books, please visit **www.walnutstreetbooks.com**.

To receive brief monthly updates about upcoming books and other news, sign up at **www.walnutstreetbooks.com/#updates**

For bulk orders of this book, contact: info@walnutstreetbooks.com

55 and Counting

A Guide for Pre-Retirement

Gerald W. Kaufman, MSW • L. Marlene Kaufman, MSW

WALNUT
STREET
BOOKS
LANCASTER,
PENNSYLVANIA

walnutstreetbooks.com

Cover and page design by Cliff Snyder

55 and Counting
Copyright © 2020 by Gerald W. Kaufman and L. Marlene Kaufman

Paperback: 9781947597327
PDF: 9781947597334
EPUB: 9781947597334
Kindle: 9781947597334

Library of Congress Control Number: Data available.

55 and Counting is published by
Walnut Street Books, Lancaster, Pennsylvania

info@walnutstreetbooks.com

CONTENTS

PREFACE

Many people delay thinking about their future during the years when they're caring for their children and aging parents. But we hope that you will take the opportunity in your pre-retirement years to give thought to your future.

We were privileged to have many persons share their stories with us for this book. We are grateful for their courage and insights. To protect the privacy of some of our storytellers, we changed some names and other identifiers. Please note, however, that the stories at the beginning of each chapter are imaginary.

We (Gerald and Marlene) have chosen to use the pronoun "we" throughout the book to refer both to our primary readers, and also to those of us who have gone through this transition. We are all in the process of aging, so we use an inclusive pronoun that does not suggest we are separate or condescending. We all continue to grapple with the changes that confront us.

1

CONVERSATIONS ABOUT THE FUTURE

I read an article that said the time to start planning for retirement begins in your early 50s. Don't you think that's rushing it a bit? We're both 55 and in pretty good shape. I have plenty to worry about with my 80-year-old parents: their memory decline and other health problems, not to mention decisions about whether they should stay in their home. It's hard to start thinking about **my** retirement while I am focusing on **them**.

I love my job as a nurse and just got promoted to supervisor in the GI unit. My husband is happy working for an insurance company. Financially, we're comfortable. Our kids are starting lives of their own. Now that we can travel and do some fun things, why can't we put off thinking about retirement until we're closer to 65?

The 50s are a season of change. It seems like only yesterday that friends and family gathered to celebrate our 50th birthdays. Even though the parties were meant to be humorous, they suggested that we were entering a new life stage—ready or not. The not-so-subtle message was that we are expected now to ratchet up our adult responsibilities and make something of ourselves while we still have a chance. Another not-so-subtle message suggested we are already old.

Although we try to avoid noticing, we do see some signs of aging. It is harder to reach our toes, and we tend to fall asleep watching the evening news. We have trouble getting used to our trifocals. We color our hair to look more youthful. We are told teasingly that we are over the hill when we drop out of the softball league or can no longer keep up with younger women on the tennis court.

We were taken off guard when our doctor ordered some screening tests, including a colonoscopy. It was also a bit disheartening to hear him say that our elevated blood pressure is connected to our weight gain. We can no longer ignore these changes. But we take a bit of comfort from knowing that some of our peers are experiencing similar health challenges. We take special notice when some of them are diagnosed with life-threatening diseases. Maybe the time has come to make some changes in our lifestyle.

What we cannot ignore is the fact that the change we are experiencing is like none we have had before. In some ways, preparing for older adulthood and retirement may be more complicated than, say, entering adolescence, starting a career, getting married, or becoming parents. Those changes were all about growth and expansion, filled with times of excitement and anticipation. Now more of the changes involve losses and endings—something we haven't given much thought to. We know we have to give more attention to our relationships, finances, and other important matters.

The goodness of life now

But for the most part we are at the pinnacle of life. According to the American Psychological Association, at age 60 we are at the most confident time of our lives. As we approach that marker, life is going just fine for many of us. Some say it's our greatest time of output. We are skillful craftspersons, respected healthcare providers, successful business persons and professionals, leaders in our houses of worship, presidents of local service clubs, and the list goes on. We are looked up to by our family, friends, and the broader community. Many people know us by our first name. We can walk downtown feeling respected.

This may be a time when we are blessed with stable finances, allowing us to dabble in the good life. We live in attractive houses in comfortable neighborhoods. Some of us take cruises to interesting places, while others enjoy more modest pleasures, like camping and summer trips to the beach. If we have children, they might be in college—some with prestigious names. Some are developing a life on their own. Life is good!

This is also the time when we belong to friendship networks that provide support and identity. We need each other, learn from each other, and have the comfort of knowing that we are accepted by our peers. Although our lives are filled with busyness, most of it brings joy. Sometimes we glance ahead furtively and imagine a time called retirement when we can sit back and relax. But we're not ready to do that while things are going so well. Thoughts of changes that might come in the future occasionally slip into our minds, but we push them aside.

Our varied life situations

We enter this important time of transition from different perspectives. While many of us are married with children, some of us have no children, or we have children but sense we can't count on them for support in the years ahead. Perhaps we have always been single or are divorced or widowed. As single people, we know we will experience some special challenges without a partner.

Whatever our situation, we are all sitting on the doorstep of older adulthood, and perhaps retirement, and can have mixed feelings about what is happening to us. On the bright side, we look forward to being able to sleep in, play golf or tennis, and travel. Some of us anticipate the day when we no longer have to put up with the annoyances and demands of our present job. On the darker side, we may have already started grieving the day we turn in our keys and go off into a world that we imagine will be empty.

We may be relieved when we hear about peers older than we are who remain in their present jobs long past the traditional retirement age. Others find new careers, develop meaningful hobbies, or immerse themselves in life-giving volunteer assignments. That is encouraging and gives us hope for the future.

Living on the margins

Unfortunately, some of us are in situations that are not so good. Whether because of choices that led to poor outcomes, inadequate skills, or limited opportunities, we find ourselves on the edge of the world around us. Perhaps we have not been able to maintain a meaningful career. We may have low incomes, or we don't get much affirmation. People pass by without even noticing us. We feel marginalized and left without a support community.

Special challenges

We may have been looking forward to becoming empty-nesters when life circumstances suddenly surprise us. We may be called on to give care to grandchildren or aging parents, some with significant needs. Many of our peers are making space for an adult child who comes back home, sometimes bringing a partner and children as well. Our view of the goodness of these years is altered, sometimes for the better and sometimes not.

Those of us who are single, divorced, or have lost our spouses through death have special challenges. Not only do we lack a partner to help carry the load financially, we also don't have someone with whom we can share our feelings and our dreams. Those of us who have always been single have found ways of coping with life, but as retirement is approaching, we may feel especially vulnerable. Where do we turn for meaningful relationships that provide comfort, advice, and the support we need?

Even though divorced persons experience some of these challenges, they may also have emotional wounds to heal, conflict to face with their former spouse, attachment issues with children, and financial insecurities. Few want to be identified as a divorced person. So now in this time of transition not only are we an "ex-nurse" or "ex-business owner," we are also an "ex-spouse."

Widows or widowers deal with some of these same issues. In addition, most experience profound grief, regrets, and fear of facing the future alone after many years of marriage. Marriage provided a role-sharing arrangement, often with one managing finances while the other handled house and car maintenance, for example. Now the survivor has to assume all of the functions alone. We may face these challenges at the same time that we are beginning to anticipate retirement alone.

Avoiding thoughts of older adulthood and retirement

Whether life is going well or we are experiencing some setbacks, our tendency is to put off preparing for older adulthood and retirement. This may be even more difficult for our generation than it was for previous generations when expectations may have been clearer.

Why do we avoid the subject? Perhaps it is the word itself. "Retirement" means ending an important phase of our life and entering a time of reduced productivity. We wonder how we will find meaning and purpose when we are no longer doing important work. Perhaps it is helpful to some of us to say "next chapter" or "post-career" instead of "retirement." For all of us, though, we can discover outlets that bring us hope, energy, and new life.

We may view the transitions of aging through the images we had of our grandparents. Many of them died before age 60, and those who lived into old age appeared disabled and diminished. Few of them worked past 65, and then they perhaps seemed to give up on life when they no longer had a job to turn to. The image of old people sitting in wheelchairs in nursing homes is not particularly inviting. We probably need to rethink our images of aging, knowing that the process for many of us is different today.

Anticipating a decline in our own health, especially cognitive impairment, is unpleasant to ponder. We may even avoid the discussion of retirement because we're superstitious enough to believe that talking about it will bring on bad endings. We hear of persons who died a week after they retired. People wonder if they just gave up living.

However, more of us put off planning for retirement because we are just too busy and life is going well. Unknowns and uncertainties are not easy to think about. So we kick the can down the road, rationalizing that we will deal with it when we have to. But if we choose to deny reality, we can find ourselves unprepared for the years ahead of us.

Different times for retirement

Of course, there is not just one way or time to retire. Some take that step the day they reach their 65th birthday. Others retire at an earlier age because they are financially able to do so. Still others leave their job due to their inability to perform with the changing demands of the workplace. The day-to-day stresses of the job may compromise their health or safety.

Other persons continue employment for many years past age 65. It is not unusual for politicians and Supreme Court justices to work into their 70s or even 80s. Business owners and self-employed persons often work longer than average. Many of us stay on the job because we enjoy what we are doing and still have much to give to our work.

On the other hand, some of us know we will have to keep working well past 65 because we have mortgages and bills to pay. We have no pensions, and Social Security will not be adequate to meet our expenses. To deal with that reality, some of us develop new skills and find work that gives financial security and personal satisfaction that lasts well past the traditional age of retirement.

> *Janice worked as a supervisor for the Department of Health for many years. The job involved lots of paperwork, committee meetings, supervision of frontline workers, and tedium. When she reached the time that she could retire with full benefits, she left.*

> *After a brief interim, she got restless. She found new part-time work at a local healthcare center. She became a case manager for young mothers who had ongoing health issues and found the personal contact with them rewarding. The interaction with the staff was stimulating, and she regrets that she didn't make this change earlier. Janice's new job is allowing her to extend her earning years and, at the same time, experience fulfillment in a new way.*

Finding purpose beyond work

In the run-up to retirement, we need to look for new ways of experiencing purpose that aren't connected with the work we do. We are moving from a life filled with demanding schedules and responsibility to one that can feel empty and meaningless. When we retire, will we pull the covers back up

and catch a few more moments of sleep? Swimming, traveling, and joining a book club look inviting, but what about the
rest of our time?

Finding purpose apart from work can be challenging if
our jobs have been our only focus throughout our working
years. When we no longer have a 9 to 5 schedule, the extra
time on our hands can seem daunting, unless we develop new
purpose-filled activities. These can include new hobbies, volunteer opportunities, expanded friendships, and new learning. These connections help us find fresh meaning, often
quite different from what we had before. We should begin to
expand this sense of our place in the world in the years *prior*
to retirement. Developing different relationships and interests *now* helps us have some structure in place when we do
retire.

Changing identity

To a large degree, the way we see ourselves and are seen
by others is shaped by what we do for a living. It is a challenge to imagine ourselves as anything other than, say, a truck
driver or a counselor. Work labels are hard to shed, in part
because our particular vocation is what we do most of our
life. Whether that is seen by others as a highly admirable calling or less so, the image sticks with us. We can't escape the
connection between what we do for our work and how others relate to us.

That vocational identity may begin to change in the years leading up to retirement. Perhaps if we're an accountant, our numbers are still adding up correctly, but younger peers know they are completing the tasks more efficiently. Or as a director of human resources, we find it harder to keep up with new legal requirements and the demands of employees. We may be able to perform our work reasonably well, but the decline in our performance and enthusiasm for the job is being noticed. In the break room, whispers can be overheard about how long we should continue. This heightens our anxiety about staying on the job. On the other hand, some of us may not be aware of our decline.

It is not easy to be objective about our performance while others are observing our decline and may want us to move on. However, we may know intuitively that we have lost our edge and that the demands of our job are changing. Some of us even prefer to leave our jobs when employers adopt the latest technology because it's too difficult to adjust to new procedures. Holding onto what was once a stellar reputation doesn't work anymore, because we know we have lost a step or two. When we realize that we are not viewed as the most sought-after doctor in town, the favorite school bus driver, or the "go-to person" to lead the company seminars, we can begin to doubt ourselves.

At the deepest level, we start having questions about our place in the world. Is this the time to search for fresh ways of developing our talents and interests—even a new identity?

This new identity can include focusing more on others and their needs. Or we may discover expanded interests and competencies.

While most of us connect our identity with work we do outside the home, some of us spend long periods of time at home raising a family and managing a household. We can find ourselves searching for a new identity, especially when our children leave home. This can be a difficult transition when we haven't nurtured other interests. Although being a parent is an identity that never ends, the demands on our time do decrease dramatically for most of us as our kids grow up.

Evaluating our work situation

Some of us find ourselves hanging on by our fingernails to our present job, either because our employer is not doing well, or we are under-performing. Perhaps we have lost passion for our work because it is no longer fulfilling or is too stressful. We are waiting for the day when we can turn in our keys and quietly slip off into anonymity. In the meantime, we put on our best face, hoping that we can make it to the finish line. This may be the time to look for other opportunities.

Those of us who find ourselves unemployed suffer from the stresses of having to search for new work, especially as we near retirement. We fear no one will hire us at our age because our skills are not marketable. Other realities like more costly insurance coverage and a reduction in wages are troubling. Searching for work is difficult, especially if this period of instability lasts several years. With these thoughts in mind, the idea of retirement seems more attractive. But that's short-lived if we know that we still have a mortgage and other obligations to pay.

We who are business owners need to use this time to prepare for the transfer of ownership to family or to others. Failing to do so leaves the business at risk and can have a negative effect on family relationships and employees. Some businesses fail when there has been no transfer plan in place.

Family relationships

A Pew Foundation study released in November 2018 found that family is what gives us the most meaning in life. The study also revealed that wealth, travel, and jobs are less important. Enriching our relationship with our children and extended family is something we should put new energy into even if they are geographically scattered. Those of us with no children can relate to cousins, siblings, nieces, and nephews. All these relationships need to be maintained—even strengthened. Whatever the situation, most of us are enriched by family relationships. The benefits that come from experiencing deep relationships now contribute to having a positive retirement.

For those of us who are married, nothing is more important than the health of that relationship. It is our most intimate and long-lasting bond. In the middle of a busy and demanding life, it is important to pay special attention to our spouse. That can include developing common interests, reviewing communication styles, and exploring how we will share our space together. In retirement, this will likely mean finding new ways of relating to each other because we will have more free time together.

In addition to enriching family relationships, we all need to continue to cultivate close personal friendships with peers. Our friends can provide a perspective different from what our family has. Friends share in our common challenges and joys because their life experiences are often parallel to ours. Getting together with them regularly is important.

Benefits of looking ahead

We are comforted by knowing that most of us still have the time and ability to manage our lives now, as well as plan for the next stage. That process is something we have done for most of our adult life. We got the roof replaced *before* it leaked and went to the dentist *before* we had a cavity. Most of us have started to put some money aside for the future. We can shape our future in ways that give us a better outcome in retirement. Delaying the start of the process may lead to bad endings later.

New attitudes

We will have a more positive outcome if we face aging openly. In *The New York Times*, Jane E. Brody reported on a study which found that choosing to have a positive view of aging is beneficial, and can even add years to our lives. This emphasizes the importance of accepting our life stage and becoming proactive in planning for the years ahead. To surrender to the vagaries of aging not only can shorten our lives but can leave us with an empty feeling and a life without meaning.

Thinking of retirement in stages can be helpful:

- The early years when we have energy and much to give to others
- The middle years when we begin to reduce our output
- The late years when others provide care for us

We need to rethink retirement because more of us are healthier and will live longer than even in the not-too-distant past. According to recent studies of longevity, more of us will live to age 100 in the future. That could mean approximately 30 years post-retirement, making it possible and maybe necessary to work longer. This extra time allows us to learn new skills, as well as expand our interests and friendships. The way we face aging can be similar to the way we handled earlier challenges. Assessing our ability to make changes and maintaining a sense of curiosity help us to embrace the stage of life we are in. Then we can experience every day as a gift.

Summary

Preparing for retirement can be one of the most challenging and rewarding experiences confronting us during our lifetime. For many, it symbolizes endings, losses, disability, and ultimately death. It can also suggest new beginnings and an opportunity to experience life in a more authentic way. Even though we have met challenges in the past, the ones we are faced with today are significantly different. They involve deep emotions and, at times, overwhelming decision-making.

In the years before retirement, we can experience the joy of good health, financial stability, and expanded meaning. We can treasure the comfort that comes from a life plan filled with expectation and hope. Reaching out to others can provide us with fresh purpose, hope, and a focus in the years to come. We will be enriched by those who walk the journey with us. So let the journey begin!

These steps for beginning a successful transition to retirement will be expanded in the chapters ahead:

- Form, expand, and maintain rich friendships
- Strengthen family relationships and resolve any ongoing conflict
- Expand interest in hobbies, volunteering, continued learning

- Identify values and purpose
- Assess health and make necessary changes
- Review finances and work at solving problem areas
- Anticipate housing needs for the future
- Seek support for losses and endings
- Strengthen spirituality
- Expand concern for others

Reflecting

1. Which family members and friends can partner with you as you begin planning for your retirement?
2. Identify feelings that came to the surface while you read this chapter.
3. What changes will be the most challenging for you?

Next Steps

1. List your fears and hopes for the future.
2. Share these thoughts with at least one person.
3. Seek help from a counselor to address difficult challenges.

2

CHANGING IDENTITY

*S*ometimes *I get annoyed by the way people relate to me. Because I'm a financial advisor, they often ask me for an opinion about investments or how much they should save for retirement. They even ask what I think about the commercials on TV advocating one company over another. Whether this happens in the lobby at social gatherings, church, or with seatmates on planes, it's hard to deal with. First of all, I'm bothered because they want free advice. But the thing that irritates me the most is that others don't see me for who I really am. I am more than my job.*

Throughout our lives, we have multiple identities. People recognize our work identity most easily. It is the one that many people connect us with, and the one we assume intentionally or by default. Identities that carry a high status, like doctor, lawyer, and business owner, tend to bring us the most affirmation and privileges. Those of us in these careers may not disengage from that work identity so easily. For example, people may see us as a doctor long after we have treated our last patient. Do we ever stop identifying with the important role that we performed for years? It can be difficult to take on a new identity.

On the other end of the spectrum are work-based identities that are less esteemed in our society. We don't get lots of kudos for, say, running the street sweeper truck for the highway department or working in the kitchen at the local hospital. When people ask what our work is, we tend to minimize the job because we fear it presents us in a negative way. Nonetheless, many of us get satisfaction from lower-status jobs even though they may not elevate our identity. How we are seen by others may not matter much to us. Some of us view our work only as a means to provide income and benefits to our family.

Working in highly technical or specialized settings may provide satisfaction because of the challenges and reputation they bring. However, these careers may be so specialized that we are unable to explain them adequately to others. When we make an attempt to talk about our work, we notice that our listeners' eyes glaze over, and they start glancing at their phones. Our identity may invite a degree of honor, but it can isolate us from people. Techies can live in a socially diminished world. They don't talk the same language as many of us do.

Homemakers

The homemaker identity has changed over the years. It is viewed with less respect by some in our society today. On the other hand, it can also be considered a luxury when one partner can give up an income for a decade or more and does not contribute to retirement savings either. Often people who fill this role, when asked what they do, say, "I'm only a homemaker." The diminishment of this responsibility has been enabled by the availability of daycare and preschool programs, housecleaning services, and prepackaged foods.

One additional recent change is that even though more women identify themselves as homemakers, increasingly men are filling this role.

Some of us choose a homemaker identity because we believe that raising children is an important mission. We feel satisfied and stimulated. As children mature and leave home, many stay-at-home parents begin part-time jobs or return to school to begin a new career. This retooling can be challenging.

We may have had multiple identities during these years. But actually, the flexibility we've learned from having had a variety of roles may make it easier to maneuver into retirement.

Public identity

All of us carry multiple identities. In fact, we may not even be known by our vocation. Some of us are seen by our neighbors as friendly, responsible, good parents, or brave for our volunteer work at the fire company or prison. We may be the first person in the kitchen to begin preparations for fundraisers.

Perhaps we are defined by our shyness, detachment, or by the ways we neglect our property. Identities often emerge from how we look and act, and how we respond to those around us.

But when we meet new persons, one of the first questions they normally ask is, "Where do you work?" Even if they start with asking whether we're married, where we grew up, and where we live now, new acquaintances usually get around to the work identity question. Some of our vocations don't get many follow-up questions if they seem boring or abstract to our listener, while others can lead to probing questions that seek free advice.

Dr. John is a psychiatrist who flies frequently as part of his research and speaking engagements. On longer flights, after other niceties are exchanged, his seatmate usually asks the "What do you do" question. He sometimes diverts the question with humor by saying, "You might be more interested in hearing stories about my dog."

When he does disclose his profession, the seatmate may
want an opinion about a troubled relative or advice about
medication to help with his sleep problem. Dr. John often
wonders if it's worth disclosing what he does, and often
decides that maybe next time he'll stay absorbed in his
book.

Sometimes work-related identities are restrictive and prevent others from knowing us in a more complete sense. Some
of us are in careers where protecting confidentiality, trade
secrets, or business plans is essential. Nothing can be shared
outside of the office. This kind of privacy can inhibit our relationships with the people around us and may cause them to
see us as aloof. It helps if we are frank with them about why
we need to protect confidential information.

Broadening our identity

The problem with job-related stereotyping is that we are
much more than what we do to earn money. People may be
surprised to know how interesting our lives are beyond our
work. At a deeper level, we are known for our personality,
whether we are outgoing, reserved, sensitive, and compas-
sionate. We can make an effort to broaden the scope of how
others see us. We are also mothers, fathers, grandparents, and
leaders in our faith communities, coaches of softball teams,
and fundraisers for local charities. These non-work roles can

be where we find our greatest purpose. We may feel the most passion about what we do in our free time.

None of us can work forever. Yet when we check out of the workplace for the last time, we may wonder who we *really are* when we are no longer working as lawyers, pastors, hi-tech gurus, small business owners, or school counselors. How will others think of us apart from the work we did? If we've been intentional over the years to be much more than our job, we will likely find that exploring new purpose away from our job is freeing. Hopefully others will experience us in a fuller way. When we expand our identity beyond our job now, it prepares us for new life in retirement.

For most of his working years, Dick was a music teacher in a public elementary school. He was loved by his students and respected by faculty and parents. The performances his students presented were always of the highest quality. In his free time, he sang in a community choir. Now close to 80 and living in a retirement community, Dick is leading a choir of peers, helping with chapel services, and maintaining his interest in birding. When visitors come to his home, he is quick to offer binoculars. He has joined a group of neighbors that is restoring a wetland on the campus. Most of all, he spends hours every week volunteering with residents with special needs.

Dick's wife Cathy was a home economics teacher and later a social worker who served persons with physical challenges. She has carried those sensitivities with her in this new community. One of her greatest gifts is hospitality, and she loves entertaining and cooking imaginative dishes. She reaches out to new or lonely residents and functions like an unofficial chaplain. In the spring, she and Dick cover the mound behind their cottage with a wide range of flowers and make sure the bird feeder is filled.

Dick and Cathy had identities that defined who they were during their employment years. In retirement, their identities have extended far beyond what they did in their careers. They are finding new ways to be creative, enjoying the freedom to choose how to share their interests and skills. They have become much more than what they did for their work.

When we are seen by others for who we are apart from our work, we all benefit from being known in new ways. We are enriched by interacting with each other in a much broader way. That includes understanding our deeper selves, including sharing our positive and negative qualities. Beyond what we do for our work and even in our volunteer activities, opening the door to our soul can reveal our most intimate self.

Physical characteristics and identity

Our identity is often shaped by physical factors over which we have little control. All of us are born with characteristics that project visual images to others. We may be much taller than our peers or much shorter. We may be seen as too thin or too heavy. Whether or not we embrace these distinctions, they shape how others see us and how we feel about our body image. We may be defined by our outstanding attractiveness, while others are lost in a crowd. Certain kinds of physical or developmental challenges place us in stereotyped boxes. Appealing body images tend to open more doors, while persons who appear less so are often passed over in the workplace and beyond.

Chaplain Dennis has been identified by his height for as long as he can remember. It always placed him in the back row for school pictures. People expected him to be a basketball star when he grew to be 6'7". He was able to enjoy playing volleyball and to use his height as an advantage. There were times, though, that Dennis wished he could hide in a crowd.

Even in the retirement home where he works, his height identifies him. He is frequently asked by the residents, "Can I have a foot off your leg?" To which he responds, "When I'm through with it!" The residents enjoy his humor and sensitivity. He has learned to use these encounters to enhance his conversations and his identity as a chaplain. His height continues to define him wherever he goes, but he's learned to make it a positive.

Personality influences

Helen has always been a perfectionist. It helps her in her job as a lab tech where accuracy is important. She gets good reports from her supervisor and feels a sense of pride for doing things right. At home, her perfectionism bothers her husband a bit, and her children complain that she expects them to always keep their rooms cleaned up. But she says, "I guess that's who I am."

She is beginning to wonder how it will feel when she no longer puts on a lab coat to work in an organized, precise environment every day. She is also thinking about how much she will miss her work when she retires. Helen knows that she will need to make some adjustments in her perfectionism at home and with friends as she finds a new identity.

To help us prepare better for the transition into retirement, it is important to understand the role personality plays in shaping us. Personality characteristics affect the way others see us. Shy people tend to be labeled as introverts and outgoing people as extroverts. Worriers are often compared negatively to persons who are unperturbed.

But these personality traits are neither positive nor negative on their own. Yet our personality does impact how we see ourselves and are seen by others. These traits influence the large and small choices we make during our lifetime. Our personality also impacts how we prepare for the older years. We may find ourselves too passive and just accepting of life as it is. We tend to put off decisions for another day. On the other hand, we may obsess about the unknowns and be fearful of making wrong decisions or finding ourselves underprepared for the unexpected.

Life experiences

Other aspects of our identity can be influenced by life experiences beyond our control. For example, post-traumatic stress disorder (PTSD) arises after a highly shattering event, such as a war-time experience, natural disaster, various forms of abuse, divorce, or the unexpected death of a child or spouse. Other life events such as business failure, bankruptcy, and being fired from a job can also traumatize us.

These kinds of experiences impact our self-image and lower self-confidence. Others may see us as a failure or a victim. Some people are able to recover and move on with their lives beyond these unfortunate circumstances. We *can* reshape our identity.

Childhood influences

The childhood environment we grew up in shapes our personality and identity. We are affected by being an only child, a part of a large family, or by birth order. Some first-born children assume leadership characteristics, while others resist the pressure they've felt to perform. The youngest child at times is labeled the *baby* or *spoiled* but may also have the advantage of learning from older siblings. Some persons who are adopted feel chosen and special, while others feel less so when they are introduced as our *adopted child*.

Identity is shaped from birth and continues throughout our lifetimes. Even though many of these images are placed on us by those around us, we often accept them as who we are. Understanding ourselves and the choices we make along the way can reshape and even strengthen our identities.

Accepting changes

Our personality and the images we have of ourselves influence how we approach the future and accept the many changes in our identity now and in the years to come. A physical image we can't deny is when we first see gray hair or wrinkles. We may have more difficulty lifting 80 pounds of salt for the water softener, or we can't get down on the floor as easily. If our self-worth is based on our looks and achievements, we will have a more difficult time as we age.

As we've said, our work-related identities also change. Even though we may be winding down our careers and have a lower profile among fellow workers, this is a time to build on the gifts that we brought with us to older adulthood. We need to begin to find new outlets for the gifts we have. Perhaps we can imagine a future in which our people skills shift from being a teacher, a salesperson, or a pastor to one where we tutor underachieving students, drive for Meals on Wheels, or expand our skills in crafts such as quilting or woodworking. Now is the time to discover how those skills can be applied in our post-work life. We all have gifts. Our gifts can be expressed in innovative ways in the future.

Summary

Identity is something we all have. Some of us are highly identified and cast a large shadow, while others go through life virtually unidentified. Whatever the case, the ways we see ourself and are seen by others is influenced by our birth personality, life events, trauma, successes and failures, and other factors.

For many of us, our career identifies us. Various influences often reshape us, sometimes for the better and sometimes not. Now, in this pre-retirement life phase, it is helpful to step back and take a new look at who we are. When we retire, we will no longer have a work identity to hold onto. Many of us will struggle to discover who we are then.

In the years before that day comes, we are wise to examine the full spectrum of features connected to us. Knowing we will lose our work identity, it benefits us to broaden our imagination and begin to put into place other expressions of who we are. If we live into our 80s and beyond, we will have ample time to enjoy other facets of our identity which may have been pushed aside earlier by busyness and necessity. It is a journey we all need to take, and, surprisingly, one we can celebrate.

Reflecting

1. Everyone has an identity. Many factors—some positive and some negative—play a major role in identity formation. List your various identities.
2. What are the identities other people have given to you?
3. Of your various identities, which one will be the most difficult to give up?
4. Which identities do you want to maintain?

Next Steps

1. Give some thought to who you want to become in retirement.
2. Immerse yourself in activities that reflect your gifts and interests.
3. Let go of activities that do not match your core identity.

3

DISCOVERING NEW PURPOSE

DIANE: *Here I am, 57 years old, appreciating the fact that our children are successfully launched, and that I can enjoy my role as a fundraiser at a local addiction treatment center. It all gets a bit tiring, but I still love it. My work is why I put on my shoes in the morning and go off to new challenges every day. It feels good to get some occasional pats on the back.*

Our mortgage is paid off. My husband and I can now spend our vacation time traveling to faraway places. I have been asked to chair a committee in my congregation that provides meals to local persons in need. My pastor says it's all a part of my calling. Maybe these activities will help me find meaning when I'm retired, but I'll deal with that when I have to. I have all the meaning I need right now!

CHARLES: *My job as a banker gave me meaning for 45 years. It provided me an opportunity to become a vice president. I enjoyed my interactions with staff and customers. The tough times in banking gave me special challenges, but we worked our way through them. All of that is over now, and here I sit at age 72, retired, with not much to do—not much reason to get up in the morning.*

Yes, I can push wheelchairs at the local hospital and serve on committees at the Rotary Club. But somehow that seems like a comedown. My wife gets on me a bit for just sitting around, and my kids are worried about what this will mean for my health. Maybe I should get a part-time job, but what? I still see myself as a banker.

Purpose is "the reason for which something exists." It presumes the question, "Why do I exist?" Many of us don't stop long enough to ponder that thought, but this question has something to do with what motivates us to get up in the morning and find our place in the world around us.

Early influences

From the moment of our birth, we search for meaning. Even though we don't yet understand what that's all about, we scan the world, hoping someone notices us. We feel valued when our parents give us affection, satisfy our hunger, respond to our cries, and assure us of their love. Our parents' smiles and touches help provide us with comfort and self-confidence. Satisfying our basic needs, both physical and emotional, is important to our development of purpose.

Years ago, when some children spent years in orphanages, many entered adulthood feeling vacant and directionless. They had been raised in an impersonal environment without adequate nurture. Many of them felt purposeless. Some children who are raised in poverty feel the same. The experiences we have in childhood can have a profound effect on how purposeful we feel throughout our lives.

During our school years, our self-worth was influenced by the relationships we had with peers and teachers. We tested our place in this expanding environment by searching for approval and acceptance. If each of these steps went well, we strengthened our self-worth. We could begin dreaming about what we would be when we grew up. Although the vision may have changed many times, we knew intuitively that there was likely a place and a mission for us.

Unfortunately, some of us never developed a defining sense of validation. As with the children in orphanages or in poverty, this lack of validation can come from childhood neglect or abuse. Some of us lose a sense of purpose from our failures in adulthood. Persons who have chronic health problems or depression often have a similar outlook, as do some who are retired. Finding meaning appears pointless when, at age 85, we are spending our waking hours sitting in a wheelchair in front of a TV that we don't even look at.

Doing and being

What we *do* is relatively easy to identify. It is seen in the work we do for wages, as well as the volunteering, hobbies, and social events that we are active in. It is evident in what we do in our relationships and in the many ways we interact with those around us. Doing can be measured, evaluated, praised, or condemned. Some of us do a lot more than others. Yet much of the time what we do isn't even noticed.

It is much harder to measure the core of our life that is our *being*. It is the essence of our reason for being. We can only make that discovery by looking inward. That happens when we pause and get in touch with our inner selves. Some of us make that happen in the middle of our daily lives. Others of us engage in intentional rituals like prayer, silent retreats, and contemplation in order to find that part of ourselves. From that internal discovery of our reason for *being*, we then set about to *do* the things we feel called to. We make better choices and have a clearer sense of purpose.

Perhaps the most significant part of finding purpose is being at peace with ourselves. When that happens, we have an inner joy that inevitably finds an outward expression. That inner peace is filled with laughter, imagination, discovery, and hope. It ultimately provides us with resiliency that will accompany us through the present and the future. This is the birthplace of purpose.

Ways of experiencing purpose in life

For some persons, the passion to find purpose is intense, while for others that feeling is more moderate. Intense persons wake up in the morning with a desire to be highly successful in their work, to be ongoing learners, to nurture and maintain close relationships, to expand their hobbies. Many of us value life in a more middle range where we can live out purpose in meaningful ways which still give us a reason for being. We may not strive to be the most sought-after musician in town or to reach the million-mile accident-free marker as a trucker.

People can also find purpose in negative, destructive ways. History is filled with stories of purpose-driven dictators, criminals, and people getting wealthy dishonestly. They may be driven by narcissism, hostility, and contempt. Their motives don't include the well-being of others. The word *purpose* can be applied to all who have a passion for whatever goals they are pursuing, whether positive or negative.

Meaning and work

Fortunately, many of us find purpose through our work. If we have chosen well, and have the ability to perform the work, most of the time we love it and it loves us back. Although all work has its frustrations and disappointments, it is a big part of what sustains us emotionally and financially.

School librarian, Margo, was recently honored when one of her students won The Honored Teacher Essay contest which highlighted Margo's influence on the student's life. In response, Margo wrote, "At times like these you know your life is worthwhile, purposeful, and meaningful."

Many persons choose their work early in adulthood and stay with it until retirement. They find it challenging, fulfilling, and purposeful. Typically their career has allowed growth and the expansion of skills and responsibilities. On the other hand, some of us have had multiple jobs changes, some of which were enriching, and others destabilizing.

Although some of us remain on a career plateau, that job can still give us a reason to get up in the morning. We may simply get satisfaction from seeing a product that we helped to create roll off the assembly line. Or we might get satisfaction from seeing a cabinet we designed beautifying the kitchen of our friends. Perhaps most importantly, the workplace is where many of us find our best friendships. That alone can create feelings of purpose.

Staying engaged at work

Even though we may have thoughts of retirement on our minds, it is not our first thought. We are still deeply invested in this moment with its obligations and satisfactions.

This can also be a season of reduced purpose. Even the most successful doctors, administrators, salespeople, and masons can find their passion diminishing. Doing surgery can become somewhat monotonous, pastors may be tempted to reuse old sermon notes, and college professors who have taught the same course for 30 years have trouble keeping themselves from yawning. Accountants have gone through one too many tax seasons.

For now, we decide to remain committed to our own mission statement: to devote our full energy to our work. One of our purposes is to be fully engaged until the last day we are on the job. We may even search for ways to do the work better and with more imagination. Sometimes that may mean cutting back our schedule or finding some new tasks that interest us. We can find meaning in mentoring co-workers who will take over our job when we leave. It may also mean making adjustments in our career when health issues arise.

Elaine and Jeff have made it a practice to periodically check in with each other about their five-year goals. Their recent check-in was especially timely for Elaine, now in her 50s. She had been in her job for almost 17 years and had advanced numerous times to more responsible positions. As a vice president in a managed care health organization, she oversaw several teams across the country, traveling 60-90% of the time to do this.

Jeff had assumed more responsibilities around the house, including grocery shopping, laundry, and paying the bills. When he took over their social calendar, Elaine realized she was too busy and gone too much. She was now open to exploring other career options.

To her surprise, she received a phone call about a possible position in a retirement community which would use some of the skills she had acquired from her present job. More importantly, she would be able to be creative in developing new programs and supporting the organization's strategic goals. Elaine finds her new job invigorating.

This job change meant moving to a new community. The move was possible because their children had been launched, and Elaine's and Jeff's parents were no longer living. Jeff could work mostly from home or access his clients by air travel or technology. He just needed to be close to an airport.

Elaine enjoys the many new friends she has made on the job and in the community, while still staying connected with former relationships. She is enjoying the new phase that their family is in, including four grandchildren between 5 months and 4 years old.

An unexpected benefit has been that her average heart rate is now 10 points lower and her blood pressure is also lower. She has more time to exercise and sleeps better. To Elaine, this is confirmation that she made the right decision to accept the new job at this time in her life. She believes that her openness to change was the first step in this wonderful new opportunity.

We won't all find a new job that brings us energy and stimulation. We can, however, deal with any workplace doldrums by engaging in purposeful things away from work.

Finding purpose in new ways in this life stage

Even though our paid work consumes much of our energy now, we can be more mindful about expanding our horizons. Most of our children are independent, so we have more time to explore other interests beyond work. This helps prepare us for the years ahead when we are no longer working.

Mrs. Smith is nearing retirement as a teacher. She has always been loved by her students and their parents. Now as she approaches 60, she feels the freedom to look for new outlets. She joined a local chorus that gives programs throughout the community and beyond. Mrs. Smith formed rich friendships with other choir members, and she feels affirmed by the applause at the concert's end. Her granddaughter asked to take singing lessons from her, filling Mrs. Smith with joyful purpose. There is definitely life beyond the classroom.

Jim has spent a lifetime sitting at a desk with a computer, developing data for a large company. The company depends on the accuracy of his work. He has found it meaningful, if a bit monotonous. His pastor sensed that Jim has relational skills that could be expressed when the church youth group needed an adult leader. Jim accepted the pastor's invitation to give leadership to the youth. Together with parents, he developed a schedule filled with adventure and bonding. He now looks forward to camping trips with the young people and relating to them at church. He has found new purpose.

Expanding our lives by starting new hobbies, signing up for continuing education, or volunteering at a local agency helps to create a new life away from work. Many of us find an expansion in our worldviews through travel. Seeing new cultures, scenery, and historical sites can be invigorating.

Beyond the purpose we get from our work and from involvement in meaningful activities, it is important to find purpose simply through our being. We treasure each moment as a gift. It can be in silence and times of reflection that we find our greatest sense of purpose.

Purpose through friendships

We are enriched when we expand our lives through new friendships, while at the same time strengthening our present relationships. None of us should navigate our pre-retirement years alone. When we are surrounded by others who care deeply about us, we are able to rediscover the power of laughter, share highs and lows, learn new insights, and be stretched. New friendships can bring freshness to our lives. They help bridge the times when we lose contact with old friends, especially those from our work setting. Purpose, however, does not spontaneously drop into our laps. We must look deep within ourselves and invite friends to join us on the journey.

Now in our pre-retirement years, intent on broadening our lives beyond our work, family, and an environment of achievement, we look for new forms of meaning. Our sense of purpose is strengthened when we perform random acts of kindness. These are usually unscripted and not part of any specific duty. This is altruism at its best.

Something good happens to us when we give to someone without expecting anything in return. We often encounter strangers throughout the course of a day and most of us, or so it seems, typically guard our privacy. Yet when we reach out to persons we don't know with a nod or a brief kind word, we can find purpose outside our traditional settings. People who sit on their front porches are enriched by the brief conversations they have with passersby.

The stories that often close out the TV nightly news catch our attention: a stranger who returns a runaway dog or picks up our bill at a restaurant; a family who comes home from vacation and finds that their neighbor mowed their yard. Sometimes on a hospital elevator, strangers reach out to each other with supportive questions and blessings. We can honor the checkout persons at a store by commenting on their names. We can help an elderly person cross a busy street or navigate a rough sidewalk. If we are looking for ways to be purposeful, we don't have to look very far. Life is, after all, about more than ourselves. This insight can serve us well in our retirement years when we may need to rediscover purpose.

Purposeful family relationships

In some cases, our children still live with us; for others of us, our children are scattered to distant points. We may have living parents, siblings, and extended families. Some of us have grandchildren. All deserve the best we can give them in terms of love, support, and compassion. We have similar genes, history, and perhaps a shared worldview. We can make it a mission to connect with family regularly. Technology can help with communication. Visits with family can become a priority.

Grandchildren bring a renewed sense of purpose to our lives because they represent the future. For those of us without grandchildren, we may find satisfaction from relating to children in the neighborhood, tutoring after school, assisting with sports teams, or teaching classes in our faith community. We can develop our relationships with nieces and nephews.

Sadly, some of us are part of families who have disconnected with each other. Sometimes that happens through lack of intention or unresolved conflict. It's worth exploring how we might reconnect with them in restorative ways. We can consider taking leadership in establishing contact with them.

When there is conflict, the solution may be as direct as apologizing to our family for ways we neglected or offended them. The process goes best if we begin with a commitment on our part to be good listeners. If we have not yet arrived at that point, we should sincerely attempt an attitude of mutuality, abandoning any parent-child or older-younger roles that suggest superiority and inferiority. If these efforts fail, seek the help of a mediator. Unresolved family conflict can adversely affect our sense of purpose.

Anticipating losses in meaning

Losing our work identity after retirement can have a profound impact on our sense of purpose. Now, *before* retiring, we should make every effort to identify the changes and possible losses that are coming.

We need to consider the loss of structure when we retire. Our whole lives have been quite scheduled until now. Going from a 40-hour work week to a totally open week leaves some of us in a lurch.

To deal with that loss, we need to create fresh sources of purpose that give us new reasons to get up in the morning. Hobbies may help, and having breakfast with a friend can bring pleasure, but we may also fill the gap by walking or cycling with someone who shares our interests.

It is important to begin doing some structured activities *now* as a way of preparing for the day when we end our paid work. Committing to one activity once a month can be helpful to us now and later.

Loss of respect

We may begin to wonder how others will see us when we are no longer working. We may have begun to sense diminished respect from the people around us. It is common for persons nearing the end of their careers to feel that fellow workers are excluding them from the inner circle. Whether spoken or unspoken, the message is that it is time for us to move on.

In fact, some of us do stay on our jobs too long. If a slowdown leading up to retirement lasts several years, it can be troubling to ourselves, our immediate family, and our co-workers.

It is helpful if we are somewhat transparent about what we are going through as we wind down. Our honesty can enable our fellow workers to offer support and suggestions that lead to a more open work environment. But sometimes we may need to turn to people outside of work to gain a new perspective.

In our community, we hear from some of our retired friends that they are now seen differently. They talk of feeling invisible. They get fewer calls to serve on committees, and people solicit their advice less than younger people's. In social gatherings, persons look past them, assuming the retiree doesn't have much to contribute to the conversation or desirable networking connections. This may not happen early in our retirement, but many feel it at some point. However, as we look ahead, we need to be committed to do everything we can to stay appropriately relevant and involved. That means continuing to contribute our time and energy to the causes we have interest in during these pre-retirement years. Although we may eventually give way to persons younger than us, it doesn't mean that we have nothing to offer. We can freely choose where and how we will stay engaged in the world around us now and in retirement.

Loss of a spouse in the pre-retirement years

During our pre-retirement years, the loss of a spouse through death or disability deeply and permanently affects us. Not only do we grieve the loss of our most important relationship, we also lose the gifts that our spouse brought to the marriage. Sudden death gives us no time to say goodbye or prepare together for the future. Extended periods of disability, especially cognitive impairment, and prolonged dying bring their own challenges as we become a caregiver. Even though caregiving can call us to a new purpose, our broader reason for being is diminished.

Loss of an adult child

The death or medical crisis of an adult child also creates an emotional challenge. Not only do we grieve this loss, but it creates a vacuum in our anticipated future. Whether spoken on not, we are counting on our children to support us during our senior years, and now that is gone. This can be even more difficult if this adult child is involved with us in business and was expected to take over when we retire. We shape part of our purpose around a future that includes interactions and dreams with our adult children.

Some of us are diverting time and resources to care for grandchildren or help children who have returned home.

Divorce as loss

Divorce at any age is traumatic. The interactions can be filled with anger, rejection, blame, and endless battles over money and child custody. It can be immensely destabilizing when we experience divorce during our pre-retirement years. Unfortunately, there is an increase in divorces among couples who have just hung on long enough until the children are out of the home and now see no reason to stay together. We and our children can carry with us a wound that may never heal, and it is especially hurtful when we carry the pain into retirement. It can severely compromise a purpose-filled life.

Business/financial failure

Similarly, the failure of our business or a financial failure from some other source can profoundly affect us at this very vulnerable life stage. We can be left without the resources we need to maintain even a modest lifestyle. The dream that we had for a comfortable retirement is now gone, even if the failure wasn't our fault.

Deserved or not, the shame we feel from the criticism and rejection from others becomes internalized. Merle Good, in his book *Surviving Failure,* says, "If we can learn to be honest with ourselves and others, we may have a better chance of surviving life's most searing moments and achieving a somewhat fulfilling life after crushing disappointments."

Recovery

During the course of our lives, we will all experience significant losses. Some may incapacitate us and cause us to lose all sense of hope and purpose. If the losses happened by our wrong choices, we need to face up to our wrongdoing and make amends wherever we can.

However, there are legendary stories of persons who faced crushing losses and recovered to move on with their lives. All found ways to treasure small things that brought color and meaning to them. We see new life when someone holds a door for us, or we are greeted by snowdrops pushing their way through the snow in advance of spring. This can be referred to as living in the moment: the times we pause to be grateful for unexpected pleasures and joys that surround us.

Some of the most encouraging stories are from individuals who overcame losses and created an even better life afterwards. At the core of recovery is the need to connect intentionally and frequently with our friends, counselors, pastors, and sometimes with others who have experienced loss. Rediscovered purpose can be an end point of failure and loss.

In the words of Carolyn Miller Parr in her book, *Love's Way*, "The meaning is not found in the facts. The meaning lies in the life experiences we bring to the facts and the interpretation we take away. There is a way to loosen the grip of a bitter memory: it's called reframing." For example, perhaps we had planned to transfer our family business to our children, only to realize they are looking at other opportunities. This disappointment fades when we discover the benefits to all of us by selling the business. We have reframed the situation.

Summary

Purpose is what we experience as an inner sense of calling and being. It is what causes us to throw off the covers in the morning to go about doing meaningful things. It is the passion that drives our choices and shapes our responses. The passions may be large, small, and in between. They may be honorable or otherwise. Purpose is what gives us our reason for being.

Purpose is expressed through our work and through activities we participate in away from our work. Some of us are more purpose-driven than others. Inevitably we find meaning through the good deeds we do for individuals and for society. Purpose demands an output and always brings a result.

Away from our work we also engage in purposeful activities. That may be through volunteering, acts of kindness, and doing deeds to make the lives of others better. During our pre-retirement years we need to take the opportunity to enrich our relationships with friends and family. These involvements will contribute to the maintenance of our purpose now and throughout our retirement years.

When we are at peace with ourselves, we have an inner joy filled with laughter, imagination, discovery, and hope. Because it is not extinguished by outer turbulence or circumstances, we have resiliency for the present and future.

Reflecting

1. Understanding and identifying your purpose gives you peace.
2. What you do for your life work can contribute to your sense of purpose.

3. Expanding your life through giving to others contributes to a deeper meaning in your life.

4. Name 3 or 4 activities you participate in that bring you joy.

5. What steps can you take to regain purpose after an unexpected or prolonged loss?

Next Steps

1. Name particular new opportunities you can think of to express acts of kindness and compassion.

2. Identify something beyond work that gives you meaning. Be sure to regularly engage in that activity.

3. If you were to experience loss, identify people who could walk with you in your quest to rediscover a sense of purpose.

4

VALUING TIME

Karen, age 55, is beginning to feel burned out. As a realtor, she meets clients at virtually any time to list or show properties, often in evenings and many times on weekends. Some weeks she spends 50 hours on her job, sometimes leading to a sale and sometimes not. Although she enjoys the challenges, meeting the demands of clients can be frustrating. Her husband has a predictable 40-hour work week and finds her schedule annoying. Increasingly, he is doing more things by himself.

Frank, age 62, learned long ago that life was more than his job. As the owner of a family-style restaurant, he had to be in early every day to set up for breakfast and stay for closing at night. His friends golfed regularly and occasionally taunted him about wasting the best part of his life.

At Frank's annual physical, the doctor expressed concern
about his blood pressure and cholesterol numbers. The
doctor encouraged Frank to make some lifestyle changes.
In response, Frank found an enjoyable job as director
of food services at a local private school. He now works
fewer hours and has summers off, giving him time to enjoy
golfing with his buddies. And Frank's doctor is pleased
with his new numbers.

Time is a precious gift. We can treat it with respect and intentionality, or we can take it for granted and waste it. None of us can fully anticipate the challenges that will come our way over the years. Some of them may limit our free time, and some may give us too much free time and no idea what to do with it. Whatever the case, we need to manage our time.

Time as a measurable resource

Typically we spend about eight hours of our day at work. With eight hours for sleeping, we have eight hours of discretionary time. Generally, we have more free time on weekends. We occasionally refer to time as though it is a commodity. We say we *spend time* as if it is a form of money. We also say we *use* our time as something we can hold in our hand and put away at the end of the day. The way we deal with time is generally within our control. While some of its use is determined by necessities such as earning money, preparing food, looking after our house and ourselves, and offering childcare, the rest of our time is, to a degree, open-ended. The medical community tells us that to live well, we need time for relaxation.

Time is a measurable resource which has limits. In our busy pre-retirement years, many of us are stretched thin by the obligations we have. Although child-rearing pressures are finished for many of us, we have added demands from work, service clubs, and our faith communities. The expectations are different now than earlier, presenting new pressures. We take a deep breath and wonder how we can survive.

For some people, time seems to speed up during these years. All of us need to make peace with the boundaries and rhythms of time and make choices that help us use it wisely.

Changes in the meaning of time

We live in a culture that attempts to bend time to make everything available all the time. The smartphone in our pocket brings us in contact with persons halfway around the world and wakes us up at 2:00 a.m. when a friend wants to talk and forgets it's our time to sleep. We use this instrument to multi-task when we're driving, eating, and with family and friends—even in the middle of a conversation. When we review our messages—both trivial and important—our time is controlled by the intense wish to be connected. We don't want to miss anything, but consequently, we never take a break.

Old-timers bemoan the fact that they used to have a less complicated life when they could sit back and relax at the end of the day. An old Maine fisherman said in 1905, "There are times when I sit and think, and other times I just sit." Now with the electronic intrusions that are part of our life, those days may be over. In our world of beeps and clicks, we may not even know what time or season it is.

Time by seasons

Beyond the clock and the calendar, we have seasons. The writer of the book of Ecclesiastes reminds us that there is "a time for every matter under heaven." That includes "a time to be born and a time to die," and "a time to keep silent and a time to speak."

Our seasons also include winter, spring, summer, and autumn. Although they aren't easily measured and we experience them differently around the world, they are nonetheless passages of time that influence how we spend our days. Winter in the north can make us sedentary. In spring, we experience some extra bounce in our feet. In moderate climates, summer is "when the livin' is easy," as the opera *Porgy and Bess* reminds us. Autumn is a time to reckon with the shorter days that precede winter. Temperature and the amount of daylight guides the ways we experience our time.

In a related way, our seasons of life include childhood, adolescence, middle years, pre-retirement years, and retirement.

We are faced with different challenges and rewards in each stage. Each has its unique characteristics.

The season of work

For many of us, the season of work begins in our 20s and continues well into our 60s and often beyond. Generally, this time is spent working away from home for income. Some of us work in our own business from home, and others are homemakers raising children and managing a household. Regardless of our setting, some form of work is what occupies a major part of our time during this season of our lives.

The 40 or so hours per week that we spend working is, for many of us, a productive and even stimulating time. We may be a painter who preserves and beautifies buildings, a plumber who keeps the pipes working, a teacher who helps children learn, a hospital worker who helps sick people recover, or a homemaker who gets satisfaction from baking a loaf of bread. Generally, the time we devote to our work gives us a sense of dignity and purpose.

Although some of us may experience our work more positively than others, we don't want to be unemployed. From the beginning of time, humans have pursued work partly from necessity and partly for the satisfaction that can come from it.

Now in pre-retirement, we can begin to reflect on the work we have done thus far. We may have remained at the same workplace our entire career or had a number of job changes. Most of us feel pride about the work we do. Some see it as a calling that has spiritual overtones, while others just feel good knowing that their time has been spent honorably. Most of us depend on our work to provide what we need to live on.

Fatigue now, celebration later

During those years when we are under some of our greatest work pressure, it is easy to neglect our life beyond work. In our most fatigued moments, we dream about how good it will be when we retire and can then make up for lost time with family and friends. We imagine going to nice restaurants with friends and booking a cabin at the ocean for our family summer vacation. We even pledge to increase volunteering at community events. We may be dreaming of cruises on the Caribbean, significant travel around the world, or hiking in national parks.

Mike, age 58, had spent most of his working years as a manager for a manufacturer. His weeks were filled with extensive overtime and pressure from his boss for results. He was a loyal employee who earned a good income and had other perks that kept him on the job. During these years, he placed the needs of his spouse and children on the shelf, which created some distance between him and them.

When Mike was called into the office of the company's CEO, he expected good news. To his surprise, the CEO told Mike that the company was being sold and he was losing his job. He felt panicked and angry, and it took him a while to get on his feet again.

During a time of recovery, Mike began to realize that life was more than work. He began directing his energy to his family and turned to his long-neglected friends for help and ideas. After a few months, he was able to find another job in management with a smaller company. Although the wages and perks were lower, Mike gained more free time on his new job to discover a new life and purpose.

Wise use of free time

When our work demands are intense and we are not able to scale back, it is important that we make the most of our free time. We need time away from work for personal recovery, for our marriage, and for the children who may still be at home. Those who live away from us deserve an occasional call, text, or visit. The best opportunities may come on our weekends.

We must resist the temptation to continue our work at home, and although an occasional work call or text might be inevitable, we need to minimize after-hours work and defend that time as ours. Bringing emotions home may also be toxic for our relationships. If, for example, we are frustrated with our boss, fellow worker, or clients, we must find ways to set aside the tensions when we leave the place.

The time is now ours, and we all deserve a better life in which we are fully engaged with our free-time partners. We can take a walk together, pick up our hobby, go to a concert, or assist each other in completing tasks around the house.

Our free time should also create spaces for relaxation. Work has a certain amount of stress that we want to release when we return home. It can be as simple as a snooze on our favorite chair. Some of us need a more structured time of recovery including meditation, prayer, and reflection. Recent medical studies are discovering the importance of relaxation in maintaining quality of life, including postponing the onset of some illnesses and extending life itself. We should include generous amounts of laughter and lightheartedness in our free time.

Our free time can also be used to enrich our present friendships. We may have a long history together and are now facing similar challenges and joys that we can benefit by sharing with each other. Good friendships strengthen our marriage and provide perspective and support to us. To bring about the best benefit, we should gather frequently with friends. Pre-retirement is also a time to create new friends and broaden our contacts with people we enjoy. These connections can help to prepare us for the changes that will happen as we all age.

It is during our free time that we can also reach out to others in need. This can truly be life-giving to us. We can tutor a high school student who is having trouble in his math classes, or volunteer to make meals for families in crisis. Many charitable agencies depend on volunteers for fundraising, transporting patients in hospitals, or reading to elders who are experiencing cognitive decline. We might not have lots of time to do these things at this point, but spending occasional time volunteering now can open ways for more involvement when we retire.

Misuse of free time

Even though some of us have significant amounts of free time during our pre-retirement years, we may treat it as a nominal resource and take it for granted. We might resist planning for our free time because we are exhausted after a long day and just don't have the energy to think about it.

Most of us admit that we occasionally waste some of our free time. We sit around watching old movies or unending sports on TV, or scrolling on our phones. After a tough day at work, we think we deserve an escape. Now more than ever, the invasion of electronic communication devices entices us to spend hours reading messages from our friends or in chat rooms with people we may not know. We probably benefit very little from seeing the pictures of grandchildren of old college friends. Others of us become virtually addicted to various games on our phones and iPads.

In addition, some of us spend our free time doing things that keep us too busy. The faux lament of our peers is often filled with stories about taking grandchildren to dance class or attending all their sporting events. Some of us text our adult children numerous times a day while they are in college or at work. Over-involvement with our children is the sign of helicopter or snowplow parents.

We complain about being too busy as if there is nothing we can do about it. This may come from an exaggerated feeling of importance that we get from being busy. Some of us are busier than we need to be to bolster our feelings of self-worth. Others just don't know what to do with their free time.

We need to manage our busyness to make space for the possibility that unexpected events will occur and need our attention. Illness, the death of a family member, or other traumatic situations will demand that we modify our schedules. In addition, if we are too busy, we may miss out on important events like a grandchild's school play, a celebration of an adult child's promotion at work, or the drop-in visit of a former college roommate.

Time management

During these years when many of us are at the peak of our careers, deeply involved in the community and at home, we need to commit to managing our free time. It won't happen on its own. Time management is based on developing structure that includes a schedule and a predictable routine. Many of us find that a to-do list or activity calendar helps us accomplish these goals. Even having a routine for going to bed and getting up at about the same time each day can be beneficial now and in retirement.

At the moment, these tools may feel stifling with no possibility of spontaneity. However, failing to put some structure in our lives leads to wasting time, which adds to our stress load. Lack of structure may cause us to miss appointments, forget where we put the tickets to a concert, make late mortgage payments, and face other preventable outcomes.

Many workplaces ask us to participate in an annual evaluation that includes how we use our time. Through this process, we discover whether we are doing well or if there is room for improvement. And so it should be for us regarding the use of our time at home.

Perhaps we should develop a similar yearly process in which we note how efficiently we have used our free time. If we list the things we do with our time, we can evaluate how satisfying and appropriate our choices have been. We all have room for improvement, and this technique can help us assess our choices. Engaging in this process with our spouse or a trusted friend builds accountability and also creates a shared future where we live out our values with fewer regrets and less wasted time.

Time management is also important to us as we transition into retirement when life is less structured. The pattern that we develop now for our free time will definitely carry over into our retirement years.

Summary

Time is a gift we all have. We may take it for granted while things are going well and our focus is on the here and now. Much of it is shaped by the work we pursue, whether highly satisfying or less so. But work is only a part of life. We can make choices about our use of free time now, which will heavily influence our experiences in retirement. The good news is that we can, by being reflective, make changes where necessary and live in ways that project hope and anticipation into the years ahead.

When we discover mistakes in lifestyle choices, in relationships with family and friends, in the misuse of our time, we still have the opportunity to make changes. None of us needs to leave this life stage with regrets. Most failures can be remedied, and an apology can bring healing.

Transparency and a spirit of vulnerability can go a long way as we move from one life stage to another. The message of hope to all of us is that as we take ownership of our time, we can expect to reap the rewards of a life well lived.

Time management is very important in helping us engage as fully as possible with family and friends. It is also expressed through purpose-filled hobbies, reaching out to others in acts of compassion, and a commitment to continue expanding our learning and worldview. This may be a time when we look inward to discover eternal values, too.

As we reflect on the use of our time, we should think about what we have learned over the years about how to steward this gift. Most importantly, how we are managing time now should lead to skills that directly transfer to our retirement. These skills can help us build a bridge to our future and give us a smooth transition into retirement. It's our choice.

Reflecting

1. Time at work and time away from work are both gifts to be treasured.
2. Being too busy or wasting time has negative outcomes.
3. Managing your time can bring you a sense of peace and fulfillment.
4. Identify what activities give you lasting joy.
5. What activities lead to your growth?
6. How can you find a balance between your personal interests and time with others?

Next Steps

1. Make a list of how you spend your free time.
2. Identify ways you can make better use of your time.
3. List some steps that you can take to enrich your relationships with family and friends.
4. Give yourself permission to say yes and no to requests. Start a list of things you would consider saying yes to, and another list of things you would say no to.

5

PAST AS PROLOGUE

My parents often talked about how hard it was for Grandpa to retire. He stayed on his job way too long and had to be let go. He was making mistakes, and others had to cover for him. Grandpa had no other life and got depressed when he couldn't go to work anymore. He started having health problems soon after he retired. I wonder if there could have been a better way.

Dad handled his transition to retirement better, but he spent too much time sitting around. Why is it that our work is the only thing in our lives? To be honest, I'm starting to worry about my own retirement. I know I'm only 58 and should have some good years yet, but I have to admit that the future looks scary. I know that I need a life beyond work. The problem is I don't know what that *life should be. The important thing, though, is that I don't want to repeat my dad's and grandpa's mistakes.*

Standing as we are on the threshold of retirement, it is important to know and understand our pasts. We are, after all, a collection of influences coming from many persons, places, and events. All of these have a profound effect on us as we transition to a new life phase.

We don't wake up on the morning of our 55th birthday with the idea that our lives are suddenly a blank slate and we can choose any future we want. It's not that easy. At this time in our lives, some 10 years or so from retirement, it is important to do an honest assessment of ourselves. With what we learn from that, we can move forward with confidence to the possibilities that await us in the future.

Our past shapes who we are today. We still have time to change our course with positive choices. This will not happen without knowledge of our past. That knowledge influences our decisions about work, retirement, purpose, and relationships. Emphasizing that point, philosopher George Santayana said, "Those who do not remember the past are condemned to repeat it." While that puts the spotlight on failure, it also suggests that learning about our past can help lead to good choices now.

Past as destiny

Even though our past has a profound influence on us, it doesn't have to be our destiny. Stories abound of people who came from dysfunctional families and moved on to be successful vocationally, financially, and relationally. Some came from homes where a parent was an alcoholic or mentally ill. Their adult child moved in a positive direction by acknowledging their parents' failures without being drawn down by what the parents experienced. An adult child can turn to helpful mentors and role models and enrich their life with good friends. Some choose to join faith communities where they feel the support of people who care for them and are committed to the values of their faith. History doesn't have to repeat itself.

On the other hand, some persons experience failure despite the fact that they grew up with successful parents who showed them love and support. Even with all of their needs apparently having been met, they made choices in adulthood that led to repeated failure. They are the prodigal sons and daughters who return to their parents hungry and lacking self-worth. The good news is that failure can be forgiven, and persons can move on with their lives. The first step is admitting that they need help. From that posture of responsibility, they can discover how to use time meaningfully and embrace life now.

Persons who influenced us

It is helpful to reflect on how our lives have been shaped by a variety of persons over the years. Beyond our parents and extended family, other significant individuals, such as teachers and coaches, likely played an important role in our lives. When these relationships are filled with positive interactions, our attitudes about the future can be courageous and hopeful. On the other hand, if we had none of these supportive relationships and instead experienced trauma and dysfunction, we are more susceptible to continuing the negative patterns. Understanding our history helps us to know ourselves and make better choices.

Influences of personality

To a degree all of us are shaped by the personality we are born with. It is, as the saying goes, in our DNA. It only seems logical that if our DNA determines our physical appearance, it also shapes our personality. For example, if we were unusually frightened of new experiences as a child, we will likely be frightened of new experiences as we age—kindergarten then, nursing homes now.

On the other hand, if we faced life with energy and confidence, it is likely that we will respond similarly today. The way we relate to changes tends to remain the same throughout our lifetimes. When we recognize our vulnerabilities, we can make the necessary adjustments. But that only happens when we take an honest look in the mirror and understand who we are. It confirms the old adage from Socrates, "Know thyself."

Traumatic events

Beyond our DNA we are also shaped by traumatic life experiences we had no control over. We might have lost our childhood home to a fire or flood. Life-threatening illnesses or accidents might have affected us or our family members. Some people suffer from abuse they experienced when they were young. The death of a parent and parents' divorce are always life-changing experiences. Young children often suppress these traumatic events, only to have them surface in adulthood. Some who go through these experiences feel the effects for the rest of their lives.

> *Susan, now 56, is beginning to reflect on how sad and frightened she was at age six when she discovered that her father was leaving the family. Even though she was aware that her parents argued a lot, she couldn't have known the impact that their divorce would have on her life.*

> *One of the most troubling aspects for her today is not being able to trust people. Susan also fears the future and finds it difficult to talk about it with her husband and friends.*

These embedded fears cause her to distance herself from him and others. She is seen by people as aloof.

Even though she doesn't like her job, she wants to hold onto it because it provides security. Susan and her friends at work who share similar childhood trauma or marital problems are now trying to support each other as they reflect on their losses. Life is not very satisfying for her, and she doesn't have the energy to look into her future.

As we interact with the survivors of such events, we see persons with residual pain and insecurity. In some situations, their trauma has left them with post-traumatic stress disorder, a disabling condition that can impact survivors deeply. This diagnosis is often given to soldiers returning from the battlefield, or to persons who were physically or sexually abused or had other life-changing experiences. Some of these persons deal with this pain for years after the event took place. The residuals of trauma can affect our health long-term and lead to insecurity and to interpersonal failures. However, we can reshape our future when we face the causes of our pain and seek healing.

Knowing and sharing the family story

We can reframe our future when we understand the profound influence our family story has had on us. Sharing our story with others can also bring healing. We will discover stories of success and failure, how family members dealt with stress, and the quality of their relationships. We may even get a better understanding about how they dealt with life transitions. For example, if a grandparent had trouble adjusting to retirement, that attitude may have been passed on to his descendants. On the other hand, it predicts well for us if he made a good adjustment to aging.

Knowing and sharing the family story is important. In an Emory University Family Narrative Project, directed by Robyn Fivush and Marshall Duke, they found that children who know their family stories—whether positive or negative—grow up to be more resilient. The transparency can be liberating.

The study gave special attention to using the family meal as a time to informally share and live out the family story. From this gathering around the table, the children, "tend to have higher self-esteem, interact better with their peers, and show higher resilience in the face of adversity." An additional bonus is that these conversations create an attitude of perseverance that children carry with them throughout their lives. This setting provides a way of being together without distractions, including those generated by cell phones. Historian Dr. Loren L. Johns says that, "Our identity and family stories are intimately connected." Openness with family stories can profoundly shape the future of all members.

Family secrets

Unfortunately, some family stories are undiscovered because they contain secrets that are kept from others—especially from children. Protecting the secrets may be the family's attempt to avoid embarrassment related to financial failures. Sometimes the secrets involve a member who committed suicide or had an extramarital affair.

Undoubtedly, keeping family secrets prevents transparency and can interfere with relationships. Living under that cloud can follow families for generations and perpetuate a feeling of mystery that is never identified. Tainted members tend to stay on the edge of society. This mystery can be locked forever in a closet of denial, and even though the details may not be known to us, it can still affect us in many ways.

Fran, now 58, was conceived in an out-of-marriage relationship and didn't know the details until recently. She did know that she was adopted, but her adoptive parents seemed uncomfortable with sharing the details. She felt different from her peers at school and at church.

After her adopted mother died, an aunt began to fill in some of the details. She told Fran that when her birth mother became pregnant at age 16, her parents insisted her baby be placed for adoption. At that time, closed adoptions were sealed and records were unavailable to the public. Fran continued living in mystery but decided to track down any information she could.

As her aunt neared death, she reconnected with Fran and gave her all the details she needed. Even though Fran feels some sadness from the secret that was kept from her so long, she now can move on with her life and experience new freedom since she knows more about her biological mother. She found purpose by volunteering in the neonatal unit of her local hospital.

Good memories

Fortunately, many family stories demonstrate openness and positive examples of healthy relationships and good problem-solving skills. Persons who grow up in that beneficial environment will usually carry those skills throughout their lives.

Russ, age 63, feels energized as he looks ahead to retirement. He has had a successful career as a financial advisor but is ready for a change. The stress he experiences during tax season has begun to take its toll. He does not want to hang on until his health is affected. He knows there are other options for him.

Russ wants to follow his father's positive example. So Russ began turning over his business to his sons at age 60 and welcomed new challenges. He joined the board of a local nonprofit agency whose mission is to support young entrepreneurs in starting businesses. Russ wants his career to be part-time and less stressful.

Like his father, he plans to volunteer at the local homeless shelter and assist some of the men in finding work. Russ and his father, now 87, often talk about the future and share ideas about the adjustments they will make as they age.

Summary

Transparency can be life-giving across the generations. It prepares us for the changes we experience and can help to make us less anxious when we're confronted by mystery and uncertainty. At this time of transition when life is filled with responsibility and intense focus, we may not even be aware of the importance of learning from our past. It is important to pause and take the long view: examining who we were at the time of our birth, as well as the influences—both positive and negative—that have affected us over the years.

Discovering our family story enables us to see patterns that may guide us in the years ahead. It is only when we have a good grasp on who we are and where we came from that we are able to plan where we are going. Sharing our story may also be helpful to us and to our family and friends. We need to take the opportunity to begin that process now for a retirement that is filled with meaning and purpose.

Reflecting

1. Understand the good and the less desirable aspects of your personality to prepare for the challenges you may face.
2. How have earlier traumatic situations affected your ability to adjust to life?
3. What personality characteristics do you want to alter? Preserve?
4. What keeps you from sharing your story with those closest to you?
5. Reflect on the strengths and weaknesses of your family story and your personal story.

Next Steps

1. Learn more about your family story. Approach extended family or friends if your parents are not available.
2. Reflect on the strengths and weaknesses of your family and personal story.
3. Begin sharing your past and present story (positive and negative) with your children and friends.
4. Embrace the positive aspects and finds ways to move past the more negative parts.
5. Believe in your ability to change.

6

IT TAKES A
COMMUNITY

*M*ost of us have heard the African proverb, "It takes a village to raise a child." I have some idea why that's important, but I am also coming to believe that it helps to be part of a village after childhood, too—especially as we get older. I've taken pride in being independent and not leaning on anyone. That has worked for me.

But I have to admit that when my husband had heart surgery, it felt good to have friends who were with me in the hospital and who brought meals during his recovery. I was especially comforted to know they were praying for us. I formed a special bond with these friends, and I want that to continue. I think about the need to reach out to each other, especially when aging slips into my mind.

The African proverb implies that when childhood is over, the raising job is done. Yet even in adulthood, we benefit from being surrounded by a village that accompanies us through the challenges we face. As we anticipate retirement and older adulthood, our community can help us identify new purpose and assist with the decisions that we will need to make.

Defining community

Throughout our lives, most of us belong to several communities. If we are married, our community begins with our spouse and extends to family, friends, and various work colleagues. If we have adult children, they may also be part of our primary community. If we are single, divorced, or widowed, we often have friends whose life experiences are similar. Beyond them, married friends, extended family, neighbors, and fellow workers are also a part of our community. Now in these years before retirement, it is very important that we strengthen these ties.

Friendships

An essential benefit of community is friendship, whether with individuals or groups. Beyond the advice they give us, our friends join with us to cry, laugh, and share our fears. They are also a part of celebrations and times of reflection. We need these friendships especially during this life stage. The words of the Broadway musical *Carousel*, "You'll never walk alone," remind us that friends will accompany us through storms and will help us to "hold our heads up high and not be afraid." That's friendship. That's community!

A lack of friendships may affect our health. Julianne Holtz-Lunstad, of Brigham Young University, found in a study that, "In the absence of friendships, loneliness has been found to increase the persons' risk of dying early by 26%— even worse for the body than obesity and air pollution." Loneliness can also lead to hypertension and cardiovascular disease. For doubters, this fact alone might convince us to be intentional about strengthening and maintaining friendships over the long haul.

Long-term friendships

While in college in the early 1980s, I (Brent) formed friendships with 14 men that have continued to the present. After college graduation, we scattered throughout the United States and the world, but soon resolved that we would gather once a year for an extended weekend. During the first few years, we camped in tents and went white-water rafting.

After several years, we found a cabin and turned to golf instead. Our conversations have deepened, and our sharing has become more personal. Now that we're all in our 50s, we sense the importance of this network to be increasing, and all of us are committed to spending time together. This friendship community has been a valued place for belonging, learning, and celebrating. We continue to "raise" each other, and some of our conversations are beginning to focus on planning for retirement.

Glenn Sparks, a professor at Purdue University, reported in the *Journal of Personal Relationships* about a 19-year study which looked at the factors that improved the likelihood of college friends continuing contact with each other after graduation. First, they needed to have begun a close relationship with each other during their years on campus. Second, they needed to understand each other. Third, it was important that they have similar interests. He found that some of these friendships remain strong even when contact is infrequent. The friends pick up where they left off at the time of their last contact.

It is unfortunate that some of us neglect close friendships while we are at the peak of our work productivity. We may set those relationships aside during the years when we are busy building our career and participating in our children's activities. Now as the nest is emptying, it is important for us to reconnect with friends. We may not have been aware of what we were missing when we were so focused on other things.

Friendships can also be hindered when we are in a high-profile career that may cause people around us to feel inferior. It can be a challenge to break down those barriers. On the other hand, we may intentionally remain aloof to prevent people from turning to us for advice. We don't want to always be on duty. Taking this position, though, can leave us feeling lonely and isolated. Friendships work best when we experience a spirit of commonality.

Mark, a 59-year-old insurance salesperson, had a reputation for being one of the most successful agents in his community. He spent long hours in the office and with clients. Even at home, he was on his computer for long periods and was fatigued by the end of the day. Not only did these work habits cut into his family time, they limited his friendships. Mark convinced himself that his financial success was most important and pushed his social needs off for another time.

After having a significant heart event, Mark was forced to scale back at work. It was then that he felt lonely and realized his need for friendships. He began to reach out to peers, but at first they were not responsive. Mark persisted and began to share deeply with them about his fears and loneliness. Finally, Mark's friends responded positively, and he found their compassion to be comforting.

Some of us avoid close relationships for other reasons. We value our independence and rationalize that needing peoples' help is a sign of weakness. Our friendships tend to be superficial and driven by work-related interests. Furthermore, we may not want to be a burden on others, so we try to solve our own problems. These choices isolate us from friendships and the very communities that can be crucial to us.

Experiencing aloneness

In our pre-retirement years, we may experience aloneness. It can come from losing our spouse through death or disability. This loss presents us with a future that can look empty, frightening, and lonely. Even though the memories that we hold onto are treasured, they alone can't fill our empty spaces. This is when the support of family and friends is especially helpful.

For those of us who are divorced, it is also important to connect with a support community. Sometimes we find it difficult to reach out to others who were friends with both spouses and now feel they need to choose sides. However, we need friends to give us new perspective and hope.

Many of us who have always been single have found ways to deal with aloneness and have become self-reliant, but we, too, must continue to enrich our lives through close relationships. Even though we may have cultivated rich relationships over the years, it is important to continue to form additional friendships. Many of us are in circumstances that are somewhat fluid. We have to adapt by taking the initiative for getting together with friends.

Marilyn, now approaching 60, is becoming more aware that as a single woman she has to give more thought to her future. Foremost in her mind is how to best maintain a supportive community that will be with her as she ages. She has lived in the same area for 25 years, so it seems like home. She has one sister nearby, but all her other siblings and nieces and nephews live elsewhere. That gives her pause and is causing her to think more about how to maintain her community in this time of transition.

Marilyn is committed to enlarging her network of friends. Some are long-term friendships, while others come and go for various reasons. Although Marilyn is confident that her faith community will provide her lifelong support, she realizes that she must put effort into building new relationships. It is clear that giving is a part of receiving. When she talks with others about her situation, she finds clarity and develops plans for the future. This reduces her anxiety around financial issues and housing decisions.

Some singles lament that they are often socially excluded from the married world. They desire to be enriched by cross-gender friendships. To enlarge their community, married persons also need to reach out to single friends and value what they offer. It's broadening for both to engage in activities together.

Marital friendship

For many of us, our spouse tops our friendship list. We share a lifetime of memories, challenges, and joys by being at each other's side in good and bad times. Our memory banks are filled with raising children and experiencing vacations, holidays, birthdays, and important milestones together.

Our relationship was shaped in earlier years by parenting and our jobs. Even though our marriage was compatible, we were often distracted by the pressures of that life stage. Surprisingly, with more time available in pre-retirement years, we may not be sure how to relate to each other. Any differences between us may become more pronounced as we approach retirement.

Many spouses approach the transitions of aging differently. One may be ready to end employment before the other. One may want to travel a lot while the other doesn't. The two may handle money differently or have contrasting feelings about their relationship. When that happens, it is important to pause and start some conversations. It may even be helpful to sit down with a neutral party—a therapist or advisor—to work out these differences. We don't want to carry unfinished business in our marriage or find ourselves strangers with little in common at this important time.

Unfortunately, some of us avoid these conversations because we don't want to upset each other. We fear casting a pall over our relationship while we are still reaping the rewards from our work. We try to convince ourselves that we'll deal with what the future brings when we have to.

Beginning the conversations may be the most difficult part.

Friendships with others

Friendships with other couples and their families can strengthen our marriage because we are on a similar journey. Being too focused on our own spouse and family can minimize contacts with others who can provide a fresh and broader perspective. This isolation can limit our individual growth and put too much pressure on our marriage. If we don't have these kinds of friendships, we should seek them. It is invigorating to find friendships in which all spouses enjoy each other and share common memories.

The Alwine, Garber, and Kaufman families formed a bond while the men were in graduate school. Then in their mid-20s, they had much in common even as they were deeply involved in their studies and raising young families. In the midst of the daily challenges of being a student, finding enough money to pay the bills, and parenting, they all needed each other. The families gathered at one of their homes regularly, learning from each other and providing emotional support. The children, too, were included in these deepening friendships. In a sense, they were becoming family to each other.

Over the years, these three families continued to celebrate the holidays together when they weren't with their extended families. They treasured the arrival of new babies and went camping as a group from time to time. They also supported each other in facing challenges. When two of the men developed significant illnesses, the families grew even closer. When death came, the survivors continued to support each other. Their shared history is comforting. The ongoing sense of being family and community is important to them and their children.

New relationships with adult children

During our pre-retirement years, our relationships with our adult children are changing. Some of us are anticipating the time when they will be living independently, launching into careers, marrying, and having children. Others of us have already experienced this transition. We carry all of the history that we have shared with them to the present moment. Our bond prepares us for the changes that are coming. We relate to them differently now that they are adults.

This is the time to broaden the conversations with our adult children and welcome them as partners as we parents face our futures. That includes sharing our thoughts and feelings about retirement and aging. It makes the transition smoother later on when they join us to discuss practical matters like our finances, housing, and health. It is new territory for us and for them. And it may be bumpy!

Grandchildren

If we have grandchildren, they can bring new life to us and vice versa. We may now have more time to enjoy sleepovers with them and other special activities. Establishing traditions together over the years strengthens our communal relationship. When grandchildren live some distance away, it takes a bit more planning to connect, but the extended time together can be special.

Those of us who have no children or grandchildren may feel some aloneness as we begin to prepare for retirement. We wonder who will care for us when our needs increase. It is helpful to cultivate relationships with nieces and nephews or younger cousins who can fill that void. We can also seek out children in our neighborhood or faith community. The times together with our family community can be meaningful and bring benefit to all of us now and in the years to come.

Relating to our family of origin

For many of us, family members are a vital part of our community. Elderly parents have much to offer us, and we have much to offer them. These relationships that have gone on for more than 50 years are rich in meaning and can still be vital. It can be a special challenge when elderly parents live in a distant community. In this situation, children need to be intentional about connecting through phone calls and regular visits.

When parents have some form of advanced cognitive impairment, our meetings with them may be more limited in frequency and duration. However, contacts with them are important, even though it may appear they don't seem to benefit from the visit. We may find true satisfaction from singing with parents or reading to them, even though they appear to be unresponsive. We reach out to them in gratitude for what they have meant to us. We don't want to have any regrets when their lives come to a close.

We also experience community through our relationships with siblings and extended family because they share our history, genes, and challenges. We can be helpful to each other throughout this time in our lives. If conflict exists in family relationships, we can benefit from mediation services that may result in forgiveness.

Summary

Throughout our lives we are all part of various communities that instruct and support us. We need them to help us learn life's meaning and to develop a sense of who we are. Within some of these communities are friendships that reach to the deepest part of our humanity and offer us cherished conversations. Our family and friends weep and laugh with us, and they help to form and nurture us. They may even help us to live longer. As we transition through these pre-retirement years, we need our support communities more than ever. Indeed, it takes a community for us to accomplish aging well.

Reflecting

1. During your pre-retirement years, how can you strengthen your ties with your community of family and friends?
2. What challenges are you experiencing in maintaining and enriching relationships?
3. What steps can you take to resolve conflict or misunderstandings with those closest to you?

Next Steps

1. Name the person who is your primary confidant. Commit yourself to frequent and meaningful interactions with that person.
2. Continue to expand your friendship circle.
3. Watch for opportunities to have more conversations and to share activities with your spouse.

7

FINISHING WORK WELL

Maybe I'll regret leaving my job more than I think, but to be totally honest, I can't wait until that day comes. My job provides a good income and benefits, but sometimes it is so boring that I count down the hours until 5 o'clock. Pushing papers is not my idea of an exciting job. I know that I should put more energy into what I do, but it's very hard.

When I retire and walk out the door, life will really begin! I dream of sitting in a boat and fishing all day. No appointments, emails, or meetings. I'll have my life back, and it's mine to schedule. That is all I need. Planning for the future? I'll do that when I have to.

Perhaps few of us have given much thought to the importance of staying fully engaged in our day-to-day work until we retire. We owe it to ourselves, our employers, and others connected to our work to give it our best until the last day. Finishing well provides us with a smoother transition into retirement. It also prepares us to embrace the 20-plus years many of us will have after ending our jobs.

We usually think of retirement as the time when we stop working. That's easy to understand because employment occupies a large part of our lives. Typically, we work 40 hours per week for 35 to 45 years. That can add up to approximately 80,000 hours. It's a chunk of time exceeding everything else we do other than sleep. How will we spend that time when we are retired?

Those of us who enjoy what we are doing tend not to think much about retirement. On the other hand, those of us who don't find a lot of enjoyment in our work soldier on until we can turn in our keys. We are on a countdown to freedom. The challenge for us is to stay engaged until the day arrives. Whatever our situation, all of us need to be attentive to our present reality and try to anticipate what changes will come in retirement. This process will increase the chance of a successful transition.

Living longer

Retirement itself is a relatively new concept. Several generations ago life expectancy was around 65, and few persons were able to even consider retiring. They worked as long as they could and sometimes up until they died. The passage of the Social Security Act in 1935 made retirement possible by providing a pension for eligible workers.

Benefiting from many medical advances, life expectancy has been increasing over the last several decades. Now, with people living on average to 78, many more people can count on these monthly checks to pay for at least some of their bills. They are able to experience some pleasures like traveling, hobbies, and just relaxing.

Living the benefits

Because most of us will live a decade or two in retirement, we need to develop a long-range plan for how we will spend that time. While some of us will delay retirement well beyond the age of 66 or find part-time work, many of us will retire the moment we are eligible.

Our plan should focus on structured and purposeful activities. Perhaps we are already active as a volunteer and can now expand our time in that setting. Others will take classes that open new interests and knowledge. Many people use this time to develop or expand a hobby, while others will serve as unofficial mentors to younger persons. Hopefully all of us will enjoy the extra time with our spouse, family, and friends.

It is important that we engage in non-work activities long before we retire. These activities are beneficial to the people we interact with, and they help us keep our focus and energy on our day job. After all, life must be broader than the work we get paid to do.

Different timing for retirement

Sometimes conflict arises about retirement when couples are on a different timetable. This may happen more frequently when there is a significant age difference or when one likes their job and is fully engaged, while the other no longer has the energy or interest in their job. Maybe a spouse left the work force to provide childcare and now wants to continue working to make up for lost time.

These differences can create pressure on the relationship. Creative problem-solving is often helpful in resolving the difference. Perhaps the spouse who retires earlier finds part-time work or assumes more responsibility for managing the household. Some will spend more time with aging parents or grandchildren. Both will need to devote time outside the home doing fulfilling activities alone or together.

When both partners are retired and together much more, it is common to experience unexpected frustrations. It is important that each is clear about their expectations of the other. Good problem-solving requires lots of conversations and lots of flexibility. In a similar way, single persons who retire before their friends or siblings may find it challenging to coordinate their schedules.

Home-based work

Because of advances in technology, increasing numbers of us work from our homes, making it possible to postpone retirement. This change has redefined the meaning of the workplace and retirement. Home-based workers have more control over their work time and responsibilities. They also enjoy the fact that they don't have long commutes to work and are not exposed to workplace pressures and distractions. However, issues may arise when a home-based worker feels pressure to retire from the spouse who is already retired and is around the house more.

Don, a car salesman, had set a goal of working until he was 70. Several months before he reached that age, he woke up one morning and wondered why he was still selling cars. Much had changed over his 37½-year career, and he just didn't feel the same satisfaction from work that he had earlier. His wife Linda, who was 8½ years younger, planned to work until she was 62 so they could both retire together. But when she learned that she couldn't receive Medicare benefits at that age, she changed her mind. She decided to continue her job until she could collect full Social Security benefits at age 70.

When Linda's employer gave her the option to work from home, she eagerly set up an office and continued her same work there. She put her computer in the sunroom so she could enjoy the nature outside her window. That worked fine before Don retired and was at home more.

Then they discovered they had a few challenges to negotiate. She might be on a phone call or using Skype with someone in India when Don wanted to start making dinner. He had to tiptoe around the house or wait until Linda was finished to talk with her. After several months, Don found a volunteer position as head cashier at a thrift store. He works about 20 hours a week and enjoys his contact with the many customers he interacts with. This change was beneficial for both Linda and Don.

Job dissatisfaction

Whether we work in a traditional setting or at home, some of us may find our work unsatisfying or filled with conflict and tension. We may believe it's too late to seek other work because our skills are no longer marketable. We wonder who will hire a 60-year-old. Left without options, we continue working to help meet our day-to-day expenses and to pay down debt. Work is something we must do until we are set free by Social Security or other pensions, even if they are inadequate.

Satisfied with work

Fortunately, many of us are in careers that provide good income and satisfaction. We enjoy the challenges connected with doing meaningful work and doing it well. Even though all jobs have aspects that we don't like, such as paperwork, committee meetings, or pleasing the boss, we find enough fulfillment in our work to be able to carry out our day-to-day responsibilities.

We may have had advancements in our careers that gave us higher recognition and increased income. We enjoy the respect that we get at work and beyond. Our workplace can be the setting where we form our best friendships. We may not even be able to imagine life without work. Retirement is something that will happen later, but not now. Because of these benefits, we may, in fact, stay in our position longer than we should.

Even though some of us stay on the same job throughout our working years, a lot of us transfer to jobs that are similar in pay and status or to escape a negative workplace environment. More often, though, we seek new employment for better pay and benefits, as well as more opportunities for advancement. When we find the new job to be stimulating and growth-enhancing, it creates new energy for the day-to-day challenges.

Entrepreneurs

Those of us who are entrepreneurs like being our own boss and having the freedom to invent and reinvent our work environment. The business we developed has our name on it and gives us extra visibility and stature in the community. We find enjoyment from creating our own product or service and from the possibility of increased income. An additional benefit comes from being able to determine when and how we retire. Many entrepreneurs continue with their work long after the traditional age for retirement.

However, being an entrepreneur, while satisfying, is filled with risk. History is replete with stories of failure when, for one reason or another, the business had to be sold or liquidated. It is important to assess the health of the business regularly and to make corrections if needed.

Sometimes entrepreneurs are able to develop a business that involves family members in leadership. Often the long-term goal is to pass the business on to them at some point. When that works, family members can be united around an important cause. The very idea of perpetuity can be energizing.

But it doesn't always turn out that way. Either the founding parent is unable to share leadership responsibilities, resulting in younger members feeling marginalized, or the younger members are unsuited for leadership responsibilities. Sometimes long-term family dysfunction is carried over into the business, spreading a toxic effect on both the family and the business. Whatever the situation, most entrepreneurs can benefit by securing the services of a family business consultant who can offer an independent assessment of the enterprise. To resolve family issues, a professional counselor can be invaluable. It's usually best for that guidance to continue on an ongoing basis.

Mentoring

In addition to the mentoring that happens in a family business, those of us in other places of work have similar opportunities to teach, inspire, and help younger persons broaden their skills. Mentoring is something we can continue during our retirement.

Sometimes that task is written into our job description or may happen informally. For example, mentoring occurs when an experienced teacher oversees the work of a new teacher, a seasoned carpenter of a new worker, or a lead pastor of a younger pastor. Coaches can mentor sports teams, older mothers can spend time with younger mothers, or an older member can take a teen from church out for lunch. In some religious communities the role of the godmother/father is important.

Mentoring can energize us. It is satisfying to see younger people develop skills and assume responsibility. It is a good bridge to our own retirement and may be a key factor in providing us the inspiration we need to maintain interest in our work until our last day on the job. Mentoring is a gift we give ourselves and others, now and in retirement.

When to retire

There are, of course, many different times to retire. Although most of us work until we can collect the full benefits from Social Security and Medicare, some work past that time because we are healthy and able to continue. Others of us may retire early without full benefits if we have other retirement income or are financially secure.

Unfortunately, we may not have a choice about when to retire because our physical or mental capacities have declined, or we are simply not able to make adjustments in our work. It can be especially painful if we are pushed into early retirement. We fear the impact this will have on our financial situation during our retirement years. Losing our job because it is eliminated can be especially painful when we are near retirement age and left with few options for new employment. In other situations, we may decide to leave our work early to care for family members.

Susan was enjoying her work and knew she was making a significant contribution to the business she worked for. When her parents began to develop health challenges, she decided to reduce her hours at work which would allow more time to help them. A side benefit of reduced work time was having more time and energy to give to her grandchildren.

Susan is surprised at how smooth this transition has been and looks forward to when she will be fully retired. She is grateful for the opportunity to assist her parents during their declining years and enjoys building memories with her grandchildren. She is also benefiting from more time to read and to watch a pair of eagles build their nest nearby.

Continual retooling

Throughout our working years, our job requires adaptability, new learning, and an attitude of openness to change. Rarely do the skills that we brought to the beginning of our careers match the demands of the present workplace. Referring to the way things used to be is usually not helpful. We must attend seminars and participate in continuing education to keep up with new challenges. In fact, these learnings may also help prevent decline in the passion we have for our work.

But if these options don't help, it may be time to look for new employment. Job changes, even in our later working years, can expand our lives and give us new energy. We must be patient and smart about looking for a new job. Unfortunately, many employers are reluctant to hire older workers because their experience makes them too expensive, and employers can be wary of investing in them so near to the end of their careers.

Whatever our situation, we must not allow ourselves to be in a retirement frame of mind while we are still working. It is easy in the latter stages of our employment to be on a mental countdown to the end. We owe it to ourselves, to our employer, and to the people we serve to remain fully engaged until the final day.

If you happen to be a nurse in the recovery room, it may mean greeting your patients with touch and gently speaking their names as they wake up from anesthesia. If you have climbed telephone poles to make repairs too many times and begin to think about the day a year from now when it will come to an end, you may want to greet the children passing by below cheerfully. If you're a teacher, you may want to look for new examples and stories that bring fresh human dilemmas, as well as resilience, to your lectures and discussions.

Some of us show signs of reduced effectiveness in the last years of our career. By now, we may be growing weary of doing the same tasks or losing energy and mental acuity. In fact, we may feel that our lives in general are dwindling in meaning. This withering effect can be our constant adversary in the countdown years.

Sometimes that weariness can be remedied by transferring laterally within the company where we work, by having new duties added to our job, or from new learning that enriches our work. Or we may choose to retire early because of changes within the job that we find unsatisfying.

Verna was an elementary teacher for 33 years and always looked forward to the start of a new year. She enjoyed stimulating the highly achieving students and finding ways of engaging and enriching those with challenges. She was always eager to connect with a group of new students. Then she began thinking about retiring, yet she wanted to work her optimum number of years for financial reasons.

But all that changed when Verna was confronted with an especially challenging group of students. Even though she was able to stay engaged and meet the day-to-day difficulties, she knew as the year progressed that this would be her last. She was satisfied that she had been a good teacher, but she was ready to start a new chapter in her life.

Now in her retirement, Verna has developed a rewarding volunteer life and visits regularly with older persons who have significant health issues. She has learned the craft of quilting, and once a week joins with other women who donate their work to an annual fundraiser for an international service agency. She also enjoys spending more time with her grandchildren and friends.

Retirement is inevitable

We will either choose our day of retirement, or our employer will.

We will turn in our keys, take the sign off our door, give up our place on the assembly line, or return the company truck. We will wrap up our relationships with clients and begin saying good-bye to co-workers. Work-related phone calls will stop, the texts and emails will decrease, and we won't be invited to the company picnic. We will miss workplace friendships. Some of the things that brought us energy from our work will be gone. In various ways, work has defined our lives, and without it we face a big unknown.

Most of us have never gone through a time when we didn't have a defined schedule, and we may struggle to know what to do with our free time. That is why it is necessary to begin preparing for changes during these pre-retirement years.

Expanding our world

Part of that preparation includes developing a life outside of work that is enriching. Unfortunately, too many of us are defined by our careers and have no other identity. We need to be known not only for who we are at work, but also who we are in the rest of our lives.

We need hobbies, expanded learning, and organizations to belong to that give us a broader identity. Giving to others through volunteer opportunities and broadening friendships enriches our lives. When we begin any of these long before we retire, we can make a gentle transition when the day comes.

Summary

During our pre-retirement years, many of us are doing work that gives us an identity, structure, joy, and income. Our job gives us cause to wake up with expectations and a belief that we can make the world a better place. Work forms an image through which we see ourselves and are seen by others. These later working years may be the most productive time of our lives.

At some point, it won't be that way. Depending on our circumstances at work, we may begin winding down emotionally well before the last hour on our last day. The job has become unfulfilling, even monotonous, and we see no way to make it better. That is unfortunate for us and for the people we serve.

That makes it ever so necessary to have a plan that brings a new approach to our job in these last years of working.

In a world that is increasingly impersonal and conflictual, we need to be emissaries of sensitivity where we see our co-workers and customers as persons. We owe it to ourselves, our family, friends, and the people we work with to choose a great ending to our careers—and a greater new beginning in retirement.

Reflecting

1. Identify what you find most satisfying about your work.
2. Stay engaged in work to the last day. Be thankful for having work that is meaningful.
3. Name some of the challenges you face as you prepare to end your working years.

Next Steps

1. List the factors that will go into your decision to retire.
2. If you own a business, where are you in the process of developing a plan to transfer it to family or to others? How will you do this so that you respect the new owner's needs, your own, those of employees and staff, and the health of the business?

8

MAINTAINING HEALTH

M y doctor keeps putting pressure on me to lose 40 pounds, exercise regularly, and get more sleep. She says that doing these things might even reduce my blood pressure. But she doesn't know how hard it is to eat right. When I come home from work, it's easiest to just put something packaged in the microwave.

And then I'm so tired from being on my feet all day at work I just want to sit, much less go to the gym.

She even thinks I should get hooked up with a CPAP machine to get better sleep. It is too hard for me to do all these things. I'll just have to take my chances and see what happens. After all, Mom had some of the same problems and lived to 83, so why worry?

In the decade or two before we retire, one of the most important things we can do is stay healthy or develop a plan to become healthier. If we want to have a better quality of life and finish this life stage well, health can optimize our retirement years. We owe it to ourselves to follow good health practices.

Perhaps we're convinced that we're over the hill already and believe that there's not much we can do about it. Aging, after all is inevitable, isn't it? Our bodies are not as sculpted as they once were, and sags are showing up here and there. Our hair is thinning, or we see some strands of gray. We may also have less energy and vitality. Our body systems aren't what they once were, and many of us are taking medications to prevent things from getting worse.

Yet unless we are burdened by a chronic illness, there is much we can do to stay well, and even to improve our health. The earlier we get started, the better.

Overweight?

Increasing numbers of us enter this life stage overweight. A little extra weight may not be a concern to our doctor, and it may not interfere with our daily functioning. But we should pay attention because of its long-term effects. Extra weight increases the potential for high blood pressure, stroke, diabetes, and the development of cancer. Some studies show that being overweight can contribute to cognitive decline. All of these things can result from not choosing a lifestyle that promotes and maintains health.

Obesity often develops over many years, even beginning in childhood. It is one of the leading causes of health-related problems in this country and contributes to early disability and death. Obese persons frequently require hip and knee replacements. Our reduced mobility can interfere with life-giving activities, causing loneliness and even depression. It can also make us dependent on other people to meet our daily needs.

Many things contribute to excess weight. First, the usual American diet is filled with high fat and carbohydrates, contributing to excess weight. We have to resist many prepared foods, deli food, and convenience food. One of the greatest challenges is rich, high-calorie restaurant food. Yes, eating out is a pleasure, but we ought to be mindful of what we order.

Second, serving sizes have increased. Whether we eat at home or in restaurants, many of us have gotten used to eating much more than we need. A typical burger is much larger than it used to be. Even plate sizes have increased over the last 40 years. We can ask for a to-go box up front and put half our food into it before we begin to eat. And we can end by sharing dessert with a companion so we're still enjoying a sweet, but in a more controlled manner.

Third, researchers understand better the role the brain hormone dopamine plays in providing pleasure and a feeling of being pleasantly satisfied from food. That connection may help answer the question of why many overweight persons still feel hungry after consuming large quantities of food. If that happens for you, you may want to ask your doctor's, or a dietitian's, advice.

Increasing our emotional connection with people, especially when we are anxious or discouraged, can help fill the dopamine void that often causes us to reach for food.

For some people, hobbies are an important diversion and can help when we feel a kind of restless hollowness. Medication may also be necessary to balance the body chemistry. It is important to understand these biological connections when beginning a weight control program. Even in our 50s and 60s, it is worth reducing excess weight to reverse unwanted health risks.

Ken managed a successful family business. He wanted to follow his father's footsteps by transferring the business to the next generation. With that process started and proceeding smoothly, he didn't have as many everyday responsibilities. That left him with more time to assess his present situation and to think about his future.

Ken became more aware of changes in his health that had taken place over the past 10 years. His blood pressure was elevated, and he was now borderline diabetic. He had also gained 25 pounds. Ken reflected on what happened to his parents after the family business was transferred to him and his brothers: his mother was diagnosed with cancer, and his father had cognitive impairments. Because of these health problems, they were unable to travel and enjoy their retirement years together, something they had been looking forward to. Ken did not want to repeat that pattern.

Ken decided to act. He began a vigorous exercise program and changed his eating habits mainly by controlling the portion sizes, while reducing sugar and high-fat foods. He lost those extra 25 pounds.

To his amazement, he has much more energy now and feels sharper mentally. Ken is determined to stay healthy. He is grateful for his improved health, especially as he observes some of his peers struggling with medical issues.

Exercise

Many of us have become sedentary, seldom exercising. Many of us sit while we work. We focus on screens and the phone and spend time sitting in meetings. Although some jobs require physical exertion, many don't have the kinds of physical activity that contribute to good health. We can't depend on our work to provide the exercise that we need.

Various sources report that people who get 30 minutes a day of cardiovascular exercise are better able to control their weight, improve their mood, have more energy, and get better sleep. It can also improve our social relationships and libido. Exercise has also been shown to delay the onset of cognitive decline, allowing more good years of health before death from other, age-related causes.

Many people engage in exercise programs that are beneficial and life-extending. However, some programs may be too vigorous and can take their toll on our joints and heart. Seek advice from an informed coach about the kind and amount of exercise that will help you, bring you pleasure, and also that you'll be able to maintain as you age.

When Todd turned 50 and went for a physical, his doctor recommended that he have a baseline stress test. The test identified some abnormalities which led to further testing. Even though nothing definitive was found, Todd consequently began thinking about discontinuing marathons. He had run many marathons, and they had given him a great sense of accomplishment.

Todd also realized that training for marathons took a lot of time. He was now ready to try a less demanding exercise program. At his wife's suggestion, they started to run or walk three to six miles together on a regular schedule. They also decided to begin strength training in a health club. Todd and his wife are finding that exercising together provides an uninterrupted opportunity to talk with each other. It is rewarding for Todd that he can meet his heath needs and enrich his marriage at the same time.

The most sustainable form of exercise is walking. It doesn't require a particular skill or athletic ability. A program of walking each day is doable for most of us. The goal is to walk briskly for several miles. If we walk with someone, we increase the likelihood of continuing the program by 55%. Walking can be a 4-season activity with some adaptations for adverse weather, or it can be done on a treadmill in the basement or on exercise equipment at the gym. Walking is an activity that can be maintained throughout retirement.

Some persons find yoga to be a useful form of exercise, especially in the ways it increases flexibility and helps us manage stress. Swimming can be beneficial for persons who find weight-bearing exercise more difficult. Bowling and golfing are good alternative forms of exercise that incorporate walking, as well as competition, and can be maintained for years to come. Some of us need to belong to health clubs for a more structured environment to maintain an exercise program.

Dental health

Many of us neglect our dental health because we believe that we are too busy to take time for the appointment. Some resist because of the cost. Others of us avoid the dentist out of fear of pain and the vulnerability we experience on the dental chair. However, good dental care is something we should seek. The Mayo Clinic has published research showing the role healthy gums and teeth play in keeping us well. Failure to maintain oral hygiene can lead to periodontal disease, which in turn triples the risk of developing heart disease, kidney disease, and cognitive decline. Everyone needs to brush their teeth several times a day and floss daily.

Sleep

To live well and age well, we need to sleep well. It is generally agreed that between six to eight hours of unbroken sleep is needed to maintain optimum physical and mental health. In her studies, Kirstin Knutson from Northwestern University found that day workers who stay up late at night (*night owls*) had a 10% higher risk of death when compared to people who go to bed earlier and typically get up earlier (*morning larks*). She says, "The mismatch between night owls' internal clocks and their behavior and environment is problematic, especially in the long run."

Some of us develop poor sleep patterns over the years. It can be difficult to maintain a good sleep routine during the day if we work a night shift. For others, TV and electronic intrusions stimulate our brain, and late food and/or alcohol intake interferes with sleep quality.

Others of us suffer from sleep apnea, a condition caused by a weakened soft palate that blocks normal breathing during sleep. This leads to multiple wakenings and breathing disruptions throughout the night. Left untreated, sleep apnea can cause heart disease and other medical problems. It also impacts our relationship with a bed partner. Many of us avoid using CPAP machines which can assist in our breathing because we think they'll be annoying.

During these years our body begins to reduce the production of the sleep-inducing hormone, melatonin. This may cause delayed sleep or poor-quality sleep, which in turn can lead to depression and/or anxiety. In addition, poor quality sleep has been shown to contribute to heart problems and cognitive decline. It is very important to pay attention to your sleep patterns and, if necessary, remedy the problem. We must give ourselves time and permission to get no less than seven hours of sleep each night.

Mental health

Even though most of us experience good mental health, some of us may be troubled by conditions like depression and anxiety disorders. The JAMA Internal Journal, published by the American Medical Association, reports that there has been a substantial increase in the use of anti-depressant medications in the last number of years, whether from an actual increase in depression and anxiety or in the increase of those seeking treatment.

Whichever it is, this information should alert us to pay attention to our mental health. For some of us, our mental dips are not severe enough to interfere with our job or daily responsibilities. Others of us are more deeply affected, leading to job loss, divorce, and other undesirable outcomes. We can achieve better mental health through counseling and medication. We can be further helped by maintaining meaningful friendships.

Addictions

Just as overeating can be a form of addiction, we show addiction in other choices we make. Those include the misuse of prescription drugs, especially opioids. In addition, illicit drugs, alcohol, smoking, gambling, and excessive sexual preoccupation can be addictive. Gaming on the Internet can be out of control. Here, too, the hormone dopamine can play a role in influencing our choices. Much of this addictive behavior is enabled by a media and entertainment culture that encourages self-pleasure.

If we struggle with any of these patterns in pre-retirement, it is necessary to find professional help, including joining a recovery group and having an accountability partner to support us. For many of us, willpower alone is not enough to overcome an addiction. Addiction excesses are harmful to us now, and the consequences will carry over into our retirement years.

Health management

After age 50, we spend more time in doctors' offices. We should all have an annual physical that includes various types of screenings, including blood tests and blood pressure readings. Colonoscopies can be helpful in early detection of cancer. We should begin health conversations with our spouse and family members and involve them in our care. It is important to be proactive about our health. The wrong choices—or ignoring any symptoms or warning signs—can bring on outcomes that will profoundly affect our quality of life now and later. Good choices and reliable advice can enhance our lives in very important ways.

This is also a time to reevaluate who we appoint as our Medical Durable Power of Attorney. This person has the legal authority to act on our behalf when we are not able to do so. Even though a spouse automatically has the right to speak on our behalf, the older we get, the more important it becomes to have someone younger serve in this role. It can be an adult child, another family member, or a trusted friend.

Having an Advance Directive/Living Will is perhaps the best gift we can give ourselves and our family members. It is vital that all our family members know and understand what our end-of-life wishes are to ensure that what we want will be honored. Some of us postpone these conversations because we want to avoid painful emotions. Skipping these conversations can have a negative impact when health problems arise later on.

Summary

Following good health practices is essential to our life now and in the years to come. If we take our health for granted and live in a state of denial, that is a high-risk choice that directly affects us and the people around us. To a large degree, we must make a choice to maintain good health. When we make wise choices, the rewards can follow us to the end.

Reflecting

1. There is still time for many of us to slow down or reverse adverse medical issues when we make significant changes in our diet, exercise, and emotional well-being.
2. To age well, we must visit our dentist regularly and follow his/her advice.
3. Our doctor will offer screening tests which should be a part of our health practices.
4. It is time to include our family or trusted friend in the management of our health.

Next Steps

1. Get 7-8 hours of sleep each night.
2. Find a form of exercise that you can do 4-5 times a week.
3. Reduce the portions of food that you eat, along with its fat and calories.
4. Follow your doctor's recommendations for preventive care.
5. Name any excesses or addictive behaviors that need to be resolved, and develop a course of action to correct them.
6. Complete your end-of-life directive and share it with the important members of your family and medical team.

9

FINANCIAL PLANNING

When my husband and I go over finances with our financial advisor, we get a bit worried. I know that we still have about 10 years of earning left. Our investments are doing okay, but we do need to put more money into savings. When we start thinking about the what-ifs, we have to take a deep breath.

We hear about all the trips our friends are taking and the vacation homes they've bought. They also live in much larger homes than ours. When we look at our numbers, will we ever be able to do what our friends are doing? Will we even have enough to retire?

The biggest unknown is whether we will need care in a nursing home. We've heard how much that costs and realize that the money we may have remaining at that

time could be gone in a hurry. The thought that we may be
unable to give anything to our adult children is especially
hard to accept.

Many of us are at the peak of our earning power during
these pre-retirement years. Whether we are a business owner,
work in a trade, or are in a profession, most of us are earning
more now than we did earlier. We may have fewer expenses
if our children are gone from home. But many of us come to
this point in our lives with limited income and inadequate
savings. Regardless of our situation, we may be tempted to
push the connection between finances and retirement to the
back burner.

Facing the here and now

Finances are complex, and this chapter cannot address all
of your specific needs. We highly recommend that you seek
the services of a trustworthy financial advisor who shares
your values and is affordable. Doing so will help you plan and
make the best decisions in these years.

Take a close look at your finances now and begin preparing for the financial challenges that will come in retirement.
Your goal may be to have strong investments, solid retirement plans, and Social Security benefits that will allow you
to live comfortably and meet unforeseen expenses. If you discover now that your finances are inadequate, you may still

have enough time to improve your situation. On the other hand, some of us may have to change our expectations for the retirement years. But we all need to develop a financial plan for the time when we are no longer earning.

Why now?

Planning is more important now than for previous generations because we are living longer and spending many more years in retirement. Some of us will live 20-plus years after we've stopped working. According to the Life Expectancy Calculator, the average life expectancy for 50-year-old men is now 81, and for women, 83 years. Given these facts, we shouldn't ignore the seriousness of the challenges that may be in our future.

Long-term healthcare insurance

Although it may not seem relevant at the present time, one of the options that we need to consider is whether or when to purchase long-term healthcare insurance. It is intended to cover some of the cost of living in an extended care nursing facility which can run $150,000-plus per year. Most plans also cover care in our homes if our conditions allow us to remain there.

The earlier we purchase these policies, the lower the premium. The costs of these premiums increase as we age. Can we afford the monthly cost of care when we are on a fixed income? What financial resources will we have to cover long-term healthcare costs without the insurance?

Do we have a plan for the end of life that does not prolong dying? Do we have family who will help with our care? Regardless of our choices, we must prepare for the increased costs of aging, especially as we decline. Some of us will need to depend on Medicaid. We emphatically suggest that you find a trusted financial expert to help you make the best decisions.

Debt

In reviewing our situations, we need to examine the financial liabilities that we now carry. According to SmartAssets in 2018, the top three sources of debt are mortgages, credit cards, and car purchases. For persons between the ages of 55 and 64, the average debt load is $131,900, and for those between 65 and 74, that average is $108,000. Increasingly, college debt, whether our own or our children's, is a major concern. Although ideally we would be debt-free by the time we approach pre-retirement, some of us will carry debt into retirement.

Some of us may not be able to resolve our debt and will seek bankruptcy. The Social Science Network found that between 1991 and 2016, the rate of bankruptcy for persons between age 55 and 64 increased by 66%. During this same time, there was a 20% increase for persons between 65 and

74. The only good news was that persons below the age of 55 reduced their bankruptcy rates.

Some bankruptcies are due to medical expenses or from losing a job. Usually we cannot predict these situations. With that possibility in mind, it is important to plan for what-ifs that can take us by surprise. That is why we need to manage our expenses and reduce or eliminate debt. Every significant financial decision should be carefully considered as a way to reduce uncertainties.

Assets

Many of us live in a home where we are still carrying a mortgage. Our goal is to be mortgage-free by the time we retire. For many of us, our major asset is our house. However, that is not the case for everyone. According to Michelle Singletary in the *Washington Post*, 44% of persons ages 60-70 have a mortgage when they retire; 17% say they may never pay it off.

We may have other assets, like rental properties, stocks and bonds, and a variety of investment and retirement accounts. If we have money in the stock market, we need to prepare for the occasional ups and downs of our portfolio. A cardinal rule is to invest in guaranteed or conservative investments to fund our basic living needs while in retirement, while taking manageable risk with portions designated for future goals.

The reality is that many of us have inadequate savings. According to SmartAsset, 29% of Americans between the ages of 50-64 have only saved $45,447, excluding the equity in their home. Even some persons with a high income haven't done much better. They may carry a large mortgage and have children in private schools or expensive universities. It is important to develop a savings plan that anticipates your ongoing needs, in addition to the funds you've put into retirement accounts.

Social Security/Medicare

Since 1935, citizens in the United States have looked to Social Security pensions to provide a dependable, but modest, asset in retirement. Medicare, an extension of Social Security, was created in 1965 to cover some medical expenses for senior citizens and younger persons with disabilities. However, Medicare rarely covers the full costs of care, making it necessary for us to pay the balance out of our own pocket or through supplementary insurance. For help with the cost of our medications, we purchase additional insurance. All of these plans vary a great deal in their cost and coverage. All are complex and require advance planning, including determining when to begin and how to coordinate payments between spouses to receive maximum benefits.

While Social Security benefits usually increase each year, the age when persons are eligible for full benefits has also risen. Currently that age is 67 for those born in 1960 or later. In 2018, the Social Security Fact Sheet stated that 21% of married couples and 44% of unmarried persons rely on these benefits for 90% of their income. With the average monthly benefit running only about $1,354, that may give us pause as we plan for our retirement years. To anticipate future needs, we still have time to increase our savings by working more years. We may also have to lower expenses now and be committed to keep a better balance between our income and expenses in retirement.

Other pensions

In years past, many persons benefited from pension plans provided by their employer. However, over the last several decades, only around 24% of employers provide a traditional pension plan for employees. To adapt to this change, the government passed the 401k program, allowing an employer to create a pension plan to which employers and employees contribute. According to Pew Charitable Trust, only about one-half of workers participate in any retirement plan. An alternative retirement plan, referred to as an IRA, is available to everyone. However, this plan is more modest in terms of how much an individual can contribute each year.

Persons who are self-employed can contribute to a SEP IRA retirement plan. The maximum amount subscribers are permitted to give to these plans continues to increase.

We should be diligent about increasing our contribution to our retirement savings each year if possible as a way to improve our retirement income. Again, a trusted financial advisor can help us determine how much to be actively involved in the management of our pension plan. Interestingly, Millennials (born between 1981-1996) are investing more in retirement plans than Gen-Xers (born between 1965-1980), partly because they do not expect Social Security benefits to be available to them when they retire.

Working longer

Since more of us are living longer and are healthier than our parents were at the same age, we are able to work longer. Forbes says that about 31% of us continue to work well past age 65. Of that number, 40% continue working because we need the income or want a more sustainable income later in retirement. Others continue to work because we don't know what to do with our free time otherwise. We may also continue working because we enjoy the camaraderie we have with fellow workers or with customers. Some of us just love what we do, and finances are not a major consideration.

Donna wanted to go to seminary but saw few opportunities for women in ministry, so she decided to go to nursing school. After she was married, she and her husband both went to college. She worked part-time as a nurse during those years and when her children were young. Later, she fulfilled her dream by completing seminary and becoming Director of Chaplain Services at a local hospital. After working there for 12 years, she moved to hospice for several years, and then accepted an offer to be Director of Pastoral Services at a continuing care retirement community.

Donna finds working in this faith-based organization very satisfying, especially the freedom to talk openly with persons about spiritual matters. She observes how this interaction affects their well-being and enables them to get through some difficult times.

When she was undergoing treatment for cancer, the residents supported her in prayer and other ways. Donna feels that when she shares her experiences with residents, it helps them to know she understands their situations and gives them hope. She is energized by the retired persons on campus who continue to use their gifts as volunteers. That choice allows them to impact other residents and gives them purpose.

Donna has joy in her job each day and has the emotional and physical energy to continue working past the traditional retirement date. She is grateful for the positive feedback she receives from the persons she interacts with. She is confident she will know when she no longer has the physical or emotional energy to remain on the job.

Unique challenges for women

Women, in general, earn less from their work than men. Women have historically received wages that are only ⅔ of what men's wages are. Thus, women have less money to save and invest.

We married women have typically been less involved in the managing of our family finances, but that is changing for some of us. Our increased participation is encouraging, considering that some of us will become widowed or divorced.

We single women must rely totally on ourselves to accumulate and manage our finances. Even though we may not have as much money to invest or to contribute to retirement accounts when we are younger, our savings and investments often increase as our incomes rise. Because we are single, many of us have learned to be self-reliant and resilient in handling day-to-day financial challenges. The good news for us is that when we have money to invest, our portfolios on average outperform men's.

Finances and emotions

It is virtually impossible to think about finances without recognizing the relationship between money and emotions. Money is an integral part of survival. It touches our most primitive self, especially when we don't have enough to pay the rent, feed ourselves, or buy clothing for our children. As we age, many of us worry about not having enough money to carry us through our later years.

On the other hand, some of us choose to live with little income or possessions. We feel some freedom and contentment by accumulating little and being self-reliant. We develop a sense of comfort by living simply and being at peace with the challenges that are a part of our lives. In fact, there are many other ways to be generous beyond money, such as volunteering and other acts of service.

Edgar imagined himself becoming a successful farmer following in the footsteps of his father and grandfather. After being drafted during the Korean War and spending two years in alternate service as a conscientious objector, his priorities shifted. He is grateful that his father told him that "this family lives for more than the farm," which freed him to accept a career with a relief and development nonprofit in Akron, PA. His assignment was for one year but extended into 35 years. He held numerous positions within the organization and worked with initiatives throughout the United States and in other parts of the world.

Edgar and his wife, Gladys, raised four children on one modest income and always had enough, buying just what they needed. Edgar walked to work and back home for lunch each day. Even though Gladys never worked for pay, he says, "She made enough out of little." She would go to garage sales and buy coats for pennies, and then donate them to organizations to distribute to persons in need. Edgar is pleased that all his children continue the art of living joyfully within their means. He has also written numerous books, three of them on board service, which gave him opportunities to travel and talk about his books.

Now close to age 90, Edgar says that his retirement years have been some of the best years of his life, except for the fact that Gladys died eight years ago and is not with him to enjoy them. He was invited to join a number of boards, Habitat for Humanity International being one of them, serving as president of four of the boards. Because of these volunteer opportunities, he could use his skills in finance, speaking, and writing. Edgar helped start three nonprofit businesses, two of which are still thriving, while the third was sold. Edgar has lived a rich life and has reaped the benefits of simple, purposeful living. He feels that developing versatility is the key to living a purpose-filled life before and after retirement.

Attitudes about finances

According to the Pew Foundation, about half of Americans are middle-class. Money brings them comfort, pleasure, and security. Although some may be enticed to spend more than they have, most handle their finances properly, which enables them and their loved ones to be freed from money worries. Many Americans show their gratitude for what they have by being generous to others in need and by supporting good causes. Although they may have times of stress related to financial strain, they've learned that these times can help develop resiliency.

Paradoxically, some persons with lots of money, the so-called upper class, can be controlled by their finances. They may be fixated on where the markets end up each day around the world. Some live in a constant state of competition and comparison. Assets define their self-image and how they are viewed by others. For some, their large houses, vacation cottages, and luxury cars give them a sense of superiority. Their preoccupation with their financial value may lead them to devote inordinate amounts of energy to the accumulation and maintenance of their wealth.

On the other hand, some persons of wealth are very generous. They establish foundations which contribute to noble causes. Many support charities through gifts of time and money. They are also sensitive to the responsibility they carry in a world of need, and so they sit on the boards of their favorite causes. They view money as something to share with others. Beyond their wealth, they are defined as caring people.

At the same time, some of us struggle throughout our adult years with financial insecurity. We live paycheck to paycheck on the margins of the broader community. It may happen due to no fault of our own, perhaps as a result of illness, an accident, or from a lack of opportunity. For some of us, finances are difficult to manage, and we make unwise decisions, crippling ourselves with debt. We may sit on the back benches of life, embarrassed by the houses we live in, the cars we drive, or the clothes we wear.

On the other hand, some of us prefer to live simply, are comfortable living within our means, and choose to be known for things other than wealth. We are active as volunteers at the fire company or by serving on committees at school or at church. In our own quiet way, we are pillars in our community.

Involving family members

While we are still able, it is important for all of us, regardless of our income, to engage our adult children or trusted friends or family members in the knowledge and management of our finances. The earlier we begin, the better off we all will be. It is important for this process to continue until our death. This involvement benefits us and may also assist our helpers to become more responsible with their own finances. Our adult children or trusted helpers need to be a part of the team that includes our financial advisor and lawyer.

> *George has known for many years that his parents were living on a limited income and assumed they had little savings. He was unsure about how to plan for his own future because he wanted to be able to help them if needed as they aged.*

Should he buy a larger house that would accommodate his parents later on, or consider other options? George decided to start the financial conversation with his parents, even though it was difficult for all of them. George learned that his parents had no long-term plans, so he was left with two possibilities: his parents could move in with him, or they could find subsidized senior housing. These conversations helped remove some uncertainties and provided all of them the time to plan for their shared future.

A financial plan

Creating a financial plan may seem complicated and daunting, but it is important to get started now. Regardless of your income level, the following suggestions may be helpful.

- Prepare a financial statement that lists all your assets and liabilities, including the names and contact information of all parties involved.
- Engage a financial advisor to help you look realistically at your financial situation. Set goals for the future that are consistent with your values.
- Update your will and estate planning. Be sure to sign the documents.
- Invite adult children, if competent, to assist with your financial situation and serve as your Durable

Financial Power of Attorney. If you have no children, choose a niece, nephew, or trusted friend.

- Place all financial records in plastic enclosures in a 3-ring binder, including life and disability insurance policies; bank and investment statements; mortgage and other loan documents; your last 2 years of tax returns; long-term healthcare policy; advance directive and living will; Medical Durable Power of Attorney; a copy of your will; Financial Durable Power of Attorney; and passwords to all accounts and websites where information is stored. Make the location of the binder known to the family members or trusted individuals who are serving as your Durable Financial Power of Attorney.
- Pay down existing debts before retirement.
- Project your anticipated monthly and annual expenses.
- If possible, increase your savings and contributions to retirement accounts.
- If possible, continue to add to your income by working past age 66 and delay filing for Social Security benefits until the law requires.
- Learn about the benefits and liabilities of long-term healthcare insurance, as well as alternative healthcare options.
- Develop an end-of-life plan, addressing life-extending wishes in your living will, whether you

want a traditional burial or cremation, and your funeral/memorial service preferences. It is important to have conversations with your loved ones who will likely carry our your wishes. They can help you sort out areas in which you may be uncertain.

Summary

Finances are important throughout one's life. Now that many of us are at the peak of our earning years, finances take on special meaning. If we have managed well and been fortunate, our income allows us to meet our expenses and provide some level of comfort and pleasure. Those of us with more limited income have some time before retirement to develop strategies to reduce debt and create assets that will address our needs during our retirement years. When we are no longer financially responsible for our adult children, it frees up more of our assets for other causes.

Whatever our situation, we need to manage our finances well and anticipate the new expenses we will have in our retirement years. This is also the time to contribute more to savings and retirement accounts and to develop a plan to eliminate debt if possible. A financial management team that advises us during this time of transition will reduce the unknowns, which can give us peace of mind.

Reflecting

1. Prepare a written financial plan that sets goals which match your values. This can become a map for living in your later years.
2. Involve your adult children or another trusted family member or friend in your financial decisions. This will be freeing for you and for them.
3. Identify some of your worries about not having enough money to last throughout your life.
4. What is holding you back from correcting the balance between your assets and liabilities?

Next Steps

1. Write or update your will.
2. Develop a plan to reduce or eliminate debt.
3. Increase your savings to give you more options and control over your life in your retirement years.
4. Consult a financial advisor who respects your values and whom you trust.

10

DECISIONS ABOUT HOUSING AND POSSESSIONS

S USAN: *I just heard that Frank and Marge are moving to a 55+ community. They're tired of mowing their yard and keeping up with the maintenance of their house. In fact, they say it's bigger than they need. Their kids live in other parts of the country, and they rarely host their grandchildren any more. Now they're going to be in a unit next door to their friends. It feels like a lot of people our age are moving to places like these. Should we join the group and have more time to do the things we want?*

JOHN: *I know all of this sounds good, but I'm not ready to become a groupie. We've had a lot of good times with these people, but being around them all the time could get old. Plus, I want to keep my shop in the basement now that I have time to really get into woodworking, and I don't think it would fit in one of these duplexes. We'd have to get rid of lots of stuff, and besides, it just wouldn't seem right to give up all the memories we have here. We don't have to make that decision right now, do we?*

PEGGY: *One of the toughest parts of being single is returning to an empty home after work. I've made a number of moves for my work and lost some of the friendships I formed. I'm ready to live somewhere where I can stay put. The problem is that most of my neighbors in the past have had children, and I didn't quite fit in. Should I just move into a continuing care retirement community and be around people who are like me? I hear these places are expensive. Would I be able to afford it? At least I'd have nursing care if I needed it.*

Moving to a new place is probably not the first thought on our minds now. We are deeply involved in our careers, balancing our budgets, enjoying our hobbies, and spending time with our family and friends. Life is good, and we want to keep it that way. We hit the ground running in the morning and turn off the lights at night with a sense of peace. We worked long and hard to get to where we are and don't need new distractions. Thinking about future housing needs has little relevance to us, so we move the subject to the back burner.

While this attitude may be understandable, housing can't be ignored for long. According to the statistics, those of us who reach 65 will have a 70% chance of living at least until 85. That means most of us are going to be around for a good number of years. Given those facts, we must give serious thought to our future housing needs. Even though we may not move in the near term, it is still important to explore the options and develop a plan that best meets our changing needs.

Importance of home

Where we live is important physically and emotionally and contributes to a sense of stability. Home is where we return to after a hard day and where we celebrate special times and events. Home in the broadest sense includes the house, the yard, the trees, and much more. The visuals, smells, and sounds of our home are deeply embedded in our minds. We carry memories of home throughout our lifetimes. By contrast, people who have no stable home can feel detached and homeless.

Some of us may plan to buy an RV and travel extensively throughout the country during our retirement years. Others dream of going from one volunteer assignment to another around the world. We may even sell our homes to be rid of the responsibility of home ownership. These experiences can be enriching and freeing, but eventually, many miss a stable home base which we can share with friends and family.

What home means to us is shaped by our many experiences in childhood. Although some of us live our entire lives in the house where we were born, most of us won't. Over our lifetimes, many of us will have lived in several homes. Some of these places created many positive memories and some negative ones.

In our adult years, sometimes we moved into larger and better houses, and sometimes into smaller places. This may have happened because of a job change, out of financial necessity, or for health reasons. We may have missed the previous home and the friendships we left behind. Moves early in our adult years were sometimes made to advance our career, or perhaps we weren't happy in our community. Sometimes we found the moves to be stretching and stimulating, and sometimes not.

At the moment, we may not need to make a change in housing, but the older we get, the more we think about it. According to a survey by New Retirement, 90% of persons between 50 and 64 say they want to stay in their present home for as long as possible. Of those, 85% say they won't need to make significant modifications to their home to accommodate their changing needs. While attachment to home is understandable, we need to be mindful of changes that may be needed later as we age.

Possessions

Even if we are not thinking of moving in the near term, we should begin to make an inventory of our possessions and decide what is important to keep. We also need to give serious consideration to bringing new things into our homes. Most of us have more possessions than we need, and that fact becomes challenging if we move to a smaller space.

Although some of us may be upset by the thought of parting with possessions, others of us just avoid the subject because we don't feel any urgency to begin. We've probably forgotten the old dishes that we've never used, just taking up space in our cupboard. Our old college course files are totally useless to us now and should be introduced to the shredder. Even our treasured books are gone from our memory and gathering dust. But we're still tempted to hold onto them just in case we might read them some day. We may instead want to give them to others or donate them to a charity.

A time will come when we, together with our family, will have to make decisions about our possessions. Many of us are deeply attached to the items we are giving up. They connect with sacred memories, and parting with them seems to negate what they represent. We may try to foist them on others in our family so we don't lose them as completely, but our children may not want the heirlooms we'd like to give them.

Or it can be especially painful to family members if we refuse items they want to give us because we don't want them or have no room for them. It is helpful to reflect on how the process is going between us and family members as we or they downsize. As irrational as it may seem to hold onto possessions, we should face our feelings of loss, try to understand them, and carefully think about what's best to do.

Don't delay this process. Start now while you're able to help make decisions, and before your accumulation of things interferes with deciding about whether or not to move. If you think about reducing your possessions as an ongoing process, rather than one big event, it will be easier on everyone. If it makes sense, invite family members to be involved in the choices, once you've made the first basic decisions. You might find it helpful to categorize your possessions by:

- Things that we need.
- Things to give away to charity and to family.
- Things to sell.
- Things to throw away.

Do we one-step it—or two-step it?

Although throughout their lives, adults may consider moving for job transfers, to reduce housing costs, or even for a more attractive community, pre-retirees have some additional concerns. As we transit through this time period, some of us may experience health problems, or find maintenance of a house and property especially difficult. In addition, we cannot be certain that our incomes will increase to cover unexpected expenses. We may decide to move to free up money for retirement.

Others of us may move closer to adult children or to aging parents. We may even entertain the thought of moving to a warmer climate, fantasizing about beaches, golf courses, and a life without snow. But for most of us the fantasy doesn't last long.

Colin Holmes reported in *USA Today* that in a given year, only 3–4% of pre-retirement people move. Of those who do move, 60% move less than 20 miles away, and 20% move less than 200 miles from their previous home. Most of us stay in or near our communities because we want to remain connected with family and friends in a familiar environment. Our emotions play an important role in keeping us bonded with our history.

Staying in our present home

The majority of us want to stay where we are because we are deeply attached to our home and community. It may be where we raised our children, welcomed our grandchildren, had holiday meals, invited the neighbors over to play cards, and celebrated achievements both large and small. In some ways, to think about leaving our house and community now seems like abandoning our history.

Remaining in our present home may be the right thing to do if our monthly housing costs are manageable. A recent report by the Society of Actuaries tells us that housing is our largest expense in retirement, whether we rent or own. Those expenses include utilities, taxes, and maintenance. Our entire financial picture needs to be taken into consideration as a part of our long-range planning.

Some of us choose to stay where we are because we still find satisfaction in yard work, gardening, and simply puttering around. We may also enjoy using our home for entertaining, and it can be a good place to recover after a hard day at work. Some of us see our place as a work of art and put our creative skills on display.

Although we can still mow the lawn and shovel snow, at some point we may need to hire someone to do these tasks for us. We also must take into consideration any major renovations that we might need in the next few years. Even now, it may be helpful to remodel the bathroom to accommodate our needs as we age.

Staying where we are can be an important contributor to our health, both physical and emotional. This may be one reason that, according to Ashlea Ebeling's report in *Forbes Magazine*, 90% of couples 65 and older maintained their home as long as both were living, while 60% of singles were able to do so. She also points out that more than half of persons who reach age 95 are still living in their own home.

Beyond the emotional connection we have with our homes, the choice we make to stay is often based on the quality of our neighborhood and community. It is especially important to form meaningful relationships with neighbors when we have no relatives living close by. But whatever our situation, we all need to have a Plan B to deal with sudden changes that require a different setting.

Jason and Martha, now in their 50s, see no reason to move from their home, even though some of their peers have already moved to 55+ communities. Their house is attractive to them, in part because the living space and bedrooms are on the first floor. They made some changes to the house in anticipation of aging, including modifying the step from the house into the garage, replacing the tub with a shower, and adding grab bars in the bathroom.

Jason and Martha enjoy entertaining friends and hosting their adult children and grandchildren who gather for birthdays and holidays or simply drop in. They treasure the memories that are being created as the grandchildren explore the nooks and crannies inside and outside.

They have begun conversations with their adult children, inviting them to help decide when moving to a smaller place might be an appropriate first step before going on to a retirement community. At the moment, the older couple can mow, rake leaves, shovel snow, and perform the tasks of daily living. When they can no longer do these things, they plan to pay someone to do them. However, Jason and Martha know the day will arrive when maintaining the property will become too big a burden for them and for their children. They are exploring a number of options for what to do when that happens.

Interim home for adult children

In more recent years, there has been a cultural shift in which adult children stay longer in their parents' home or return for a season. According to Motley Fool, recently one-third of young adults ages 18-34 were living with their parents. They may be paying off debts or saving for a down payment on a house. They may be recovering from a job loss, health crisis, divorce, or financial problems.

This arrangement can provide an opportunity for parents and an adult child to deepen their relationship. But there should be an agreed-upon end point to prevent all parties from becoming dependent on each other. Some of these arrangements are more positive than others.

Rod and Jeanine, in their middle 50s, were enjoying their empty nest after their three children married and established careers. But when their son Luke and his wife Yesenia talked with them about moving back home, the answer for Rod and Jeanine was easy: Yes. They knew they would enjoy Luke's and Yesenia's companionship and felt good about giving them the opportunity to save for a down payment on a house.

Luke and Yesenia found employment in the community and moved in with Rod and Jeanine, occupying two rooms in the back of the house. All of them are relaxed about the use of common space and meal preparation. They share some meals; other times everyone is on their own. Rod and Luke especially enjoy preparing meals together. Luke is available to help with household chores that Rod finds challenging because of his physical limitations.

Rod and Jeanine were happy as a one-couple household. They are also happy having Luke and Yesenia live with them. They enjoy having Yesenia's 10-year-old twin siblings come to visit, bringing fresh energy to the house. Even though there is no definite end date in place, they do have ongoing conversations from time to time about how things are going for all of them.

Sharing our home temporarily with aging parents?

As the population of people in their eighties and nineties increases, we need to address each individual housing situation in creative ways. Many can no longer live at home safely and may not have the resources to live in institutional housing. The best solution for some of us is to live with an adult child as we age. This time together can strengthen the bond between the generations and allow the parent to maintain some independence and a sense of dignity. This plan may not work for everyone and, for those who make this choice, all close family members need to be a part of the decision.

Changes to the house may have to be made to accommodate the parents' needs. Healthcare professionals can help to identify the modifications that are necessary. To make this arrangement work, all parties involved should have ongoing conversations about expectations, financial implications, and plans for long-term care needs.

Evelyn at age 93 was living in her own apartment. She was no longer driving, so she needed transportation for groceries and doctor appointments. Evelyn was managing quite well until she was prescribed a new medication which caused some weakness and confusion. Her daughter and son-in-law, in their 50s, became concerned after receiving several late-night phone calls for help from her. They were able to alert the doctor who discontinued the medication.

This did, however, spark some discussions about a possible move. Her son-in-law suggested she move in with them, knowing she did not want to move to a retirement care facility. Evelyn agreed. They converted their dining room into a bedroom and later, after hip surgery, installed a stair lift so she could get to the second floor for a shower.

Evelyn has a TV in her room so she can watch her favorite shows. She can get her own breakfast and lunch; the family shares the evening meal together. Even though they have all given up some degree of privacy, this arrangement is working well. They have had some discussions about long-term care options when Evelyn can no longer care for herself.

Moving closer to adult children and their families?

Some of us may have the opportunity to leave our present home to be near an adult child and their family, making it possible to build relationships with our grandchildren and offer assistance to their parents. It can be helpful if we have made numerous visits to their home and are acquainted with their community. After settling in, it will be important to establish friendships of our own and find a job or volunteer opportunities. But before making this decision, we want to know that our adult children will be putting down roots and staying in that community.

Ivan and Cheryl had a successful business in the sunny South where they were enjoying living. When their three adult children married and established careers some 1000 miles away, they encouraged their parents to move closer to them. Ivan and Cheryl made frequent visits to see them in the Midwest, but greatly increased their visits after their first grandchild was born. Because Ivan and Cheryl lived most of their adult years away from their extended families, they decided to change the pattern by moving closer to their own children and grandchildren. They wanted to be more involved in their family's lives.

Knowing that it might be complicated to sell a house and a business at the same time, they met with a business consultant to map out a plan. They decided to sell the house first so they would have a source of income until the business sold. After selling their house, Ivan and Cheryl downsized and moved their belongings into storage near their children in the Midwest. Fortunately, it didn't take long to find a buyer for the business. They then moved into their daughter's basement temporarily to give themselves time to decide if they wanted to buy or rent.

Even though the move meant leaving a warm climate for cold winters, Ivan and Cheryl are enjoying the changing seasons. They miss their long-term friends and the church community that they left behind, but care most about being close to family. That fact was confirmed when one of their daughters experienced a ruptured brain aneurysm. Cheryl was able to be with her right away. Cheryl and Ivan now provide assistance as she continues to recover. Their decision to move near to their family was further confirmed when they were able to attend the recital of a niece who also lives nearby, something they were never able to do before. The memories Ivan and Cheryl are building with their family are priceless.

Long-term shared housing?

Co-housing, also known as multi-family living, is catching the interest of some people in pre-retirement. In this arrangement, the parents in pre-retirement and their adult children share a home. Already common in some ethnic groups, co-housing is beginning to expand into the mainstream. New multiple-generation homes are being built in many communities. Sometimes adult children take the initiative to expand their home to accommodate their parents as they near retirement.

Depending on how it is organized, co-housing may be economically beneficial, and it can provide a ready-made setting where grandparents can be an active part of their adult children's own family. Anyone considering this must explore the financial implications and the future care of the elders to ensure that co-housing is the best choice for the entire family. It is also important that the older generation establishes a meaningful life outside the shared home.

Some single persons are finding co-housing to be an affordable option and a way to reduce loneliness.

Moving to a community away from family?

If we are single or married without children, we may choose to move to a new location away from family. We may move because we're drawn to a warmer climate, university setting, or mountain environment where we can hike and breathe fresh air. In many of these settings, we may be able to find new employment or volunteer opportunities. Even those of us who have adult children may do the same because they are busy with their lives, or we wouldn't be comfortable living in their community.

If you're considering this, you may want to check the access you and your family will have to airports, cars, and trains to allow for frequent visiting.

Deciding to move to a community at a distance from family and friends should be done thoughtfully. You may want to think about the following questions provided by *newretirement.com* before you start the process:

- Will you be able to maintain long-term friendships that are still important to you?
- If you have adult children and grandchildren, will the move strengthen or weaken the relationship you have with them?
- If you're active in a faith community, will you be able to connect with a new congregation?
- Can you find a medical provider who continues the level of care you need?

- Can you navigate traffic challenges in the new setting? Is public transit available?
- Are costs of living, a new house, and moving expenses within your budget?
- Should you consider renting for a year to be sure this is the right decision?

Downsizing choices and considerations

Some of us who move do so to reduce the time, energy, and cost that our present property requires. The yard is beginning to look bigger than before and the snow deeper. On the inside, housecleaning has become burdensome, especially for spaces that we no longer use. Moving to a 55+ development or to a Continuing Care Retirement Community that provides a maintenance-free lifestyle begins to look more appealing. We're attracted by the possibility of having more free time on our hands. If we prefer not to live in a planned community, there are lots of choices available to us for smaller, user-friendly housing.

Another factor influencing our decision to downsize is the ongoing cost of maintaining our property. Perhaps the taxes are high, and the heating and cooling expenses are heavy. When we take a close look at our driveway or roof, we know that repairs are coming. We may also want to move to a smaller place either to reduce our mortgage or to eliminate it. Even though our new home may not accommodate the family on holidays, our smaller place may open the opportunity for our adult children to begin hosting. We may also find other venues for the family celebrations.

Upsizing choices and considerations

Although upsizing is less common, some of us move to a larger home or add onto our present home as we approach retirement. We may choose to do this if our home is too small for our present needs or lacks the amenities we prefer. We may upsize to provide more space for family gatherings and entertaining friends. A study done by Merrill Lynch found that 30% of those who moved into a larger home did so for young adults who are returning home or to accommodate aging parents.

The following points may help us to arrive at the best decision about upsizing:

- Can we afford an increase in our mortgage, taxes, upkeep, and utilities?
- Will we need to adjust our budget to match our income in retirement?
- Can this larger house accommodate us in the years to come?
- Do we have a plan for our care as our needs increase? Who would give that care and where?
- Can we afford long-term healthcare insurance that would cover medical expenses when we are no longer able to care for ourselves?

Summary

The homes we live in and the neighborhoods that surround us help to define who we are, from childhood into pre-retirement. "Home" may now take on new meaning as we contemplate the changes we know will come at one point or another.

If we stay in our present home, it may be necessary to make modifications. If we move, we need to give thought to affordability, access to adult children, connections to parents who may still be living, and the continuation of friendships and other social involvements we've had. It is important to think seriously about our housing options because many of us will have 20+ retirement years. As married persons or as singles, we need multiple conversations with family and friends to help us decide what the best options are.

Reflecting

1. Understanding your emotional connection with home is important.
2. What conversations should you consider having with your family or friends about moving or staying?
3. How are you enriching your lives with friendships and activities in your present community? Will you be able to maintain these or develop new relationships in a new community?

4. What is keeping you from beginning to sort through your possessions?

Next Steps

1. Assess your housing costs now and project possible housing changes and their costs for your retirement.
2. Collect information about housing options that match your financial realities and your values.
3. Reduce your possessions by getting rid of things you haven't used or worn in a year.

11

A SMOOTH TRANSITION

've had a good life so far. I'm enjoying my work and the respect it gives me. I'm grateful for being able to live in a comfortable house in a wonderful neighborhood. My marriage, the kids, and the grandchildren are the center of my life. I am enriched by deep friendships that bring joy in good times and support in tough times.

*Most of all, I feel satisfaction from knowing that my life is a part of something much bigger and extends beyond the present. I know if I am blessed with more years, new life will develop—a time when **being** is as important as **doing**. The toughest part is the feeling of giving in to the passage of time. I want to continue to do everything that I can in these years that are left before my retirement to adequately prepare for both the rewards and the uncertainties that come with aging.*

Think of these years as an *intermission*—when we intentionally assess our situation and develop understandings that will help us make good decisions for what's ahead. Our journey has been purpose-filled. We can continue to find and define new purposes.

When we (the authors) were in the pre-retirement stage, we were deeply involved in a counseling practice while giving time to board service, church activities, family commitments, travel, and running a household. It was engaging and challenging. At the end of the day, for the most part, we felt that we had used our time purposefully. We had frustrations and even failures, but neither of us suffered from boredom! Tomorrow was just a few hours away, but in many ways, we didn't give much thought to the next stage of our lives.

All of that changed when, at age 66, Jerry needed urgent stomach surgery and had a long time of recovery. Not only did that place limits on our counseling practice, but it also raised questions about our future. Only then did we begin to think seriously about ending our counseling practice and start to imagine the next chapter of our lives. We also cultivated and expanded friendships and spent more time visiting persons with health challenges. Our daily two- to three-mile walks became more important than ever, especially enriching when we hiked in the mountains and by streams. Freed from the daily responsibilities of work, we were able to increase our time with family. Most importantly, we found it essential to accept and celebrate this new life stage.

All of this may seem premature and irrelevant while we are in the midst of enriching experiences. Most of us feel satisfaction from achievements at work, relationships with family and friends, and our involvement in the community. We know that in one way or another we are making a difference in our world. Life is good, and we want to keep it that way.

The good news is that we can discover a new life. We can take comfort from knowing that if we handled transitions well in the past, we have a good chance of doing that now.

Images of aging

One of our biggest concerns about aging may be losing our youthful appearance. We get a temporary boost when people tell us that we look younger than our age! In truth, we admit that the physical changes that come with age are not welcomed. The good news is that many of us are healthy and we'll have more good years ahead of us. Being active and having a positive spirit is something we can choose.

Watch for persons who are older than we are who are happy, content, and doing quite well. These individuals have found new satisfaction through their current activities and relationships. They don't sit around feeling sorry for themselves or waiting for the end to come.

Expanding purpose as we age

Resist believing that your meaningful life is over and all that lies ahead is the status quo. Find something new to watch on TV, take your time reading interesting news, try new food for breakfast, call friends you haven't seen in a long time. These kinds of simple changes can bring freshness. Routine can be the enemy of growth. Getting started on these life-changing alterations helps to prepare us for a better future.

Strengthening relationships with family and friends

Perhaps most important is maintaining a strong marriage and a close relationship with our children, siblings, and extended family. For those of us without children, it is critical to connect with family and friends. We can focus on giving the people we care about full attention, listening well, and speaking words of affirmation and encouragement. Now is the best time to find resolution if we have unsettled conflicts with family or friends. This is our opportunity to strengthen relationships, seek forgiveness, and spend time together— what most of us identify as our top priorities.

Schedule regular get-togethers with friends. These experiences provide a sense of continuity and establish bonds that keep us together over the years. Friendships are the strongest and healthiest when members are transparent and vulnerable with each other about things that really matter.

Ed has been a lawyer for most of his adult years. His practice is focused primarily on real estate, especially the transfer of farm assets from one generation to another. Ed projects a certain professional image with clients and colleagues; in fact, he carries that image with him even outside the office.

Now, as he is nearing retirement, he feels freer to relate to others in a new way. He calls it taking down his filters. He is experiencing the joy of transparency with family and friends. It even helps him to be friendly with individuals he meets in casual settings like elevators or grocery lines. He likes the new Ed.

Losses and resiliency

In the middle of all these changes, we discover how essential it is to expand our ability to adjust to changes, to become more resilient. Over the years, most of us have faced adversities of some kind—from health challenges, to financial losses, to the deaths of family members or close friends. A challenging aspect of any loss is that it makes us feel more vulnerable to the unexpected. While we may each handle adversity differently, none of us can escape its impact.

*For us (the authors) our most challenging time was in
1980 when we bought a house in a new location before
we sold the house we were living in. We assumed, as most
persons did at that time, that the house would sell quickly.
Unfortunately, this was at the beginning of a housing crisis
in this country when the market collapsed, leaving us stuck
with two house payments for three years. The interest rate
for the new house was 16%, coupled with a 20% swing
loan to cover the anticipated equity that would be applied
when the previous house sold.*

*Needless to say, this situation tested our coping skills and
our marital relationship and impacted our four children.
We struggled to meet our financial obligations each
month. Buying new basketball and hockey shoes for our
children produced anxiety that we couldn't hide. We all
celebrated when the old house sold. It took years for us to
recover financially, and we had a second celebration when
we were able to pay off the mortgage early.*

*Those difficult years helped us to re-evaluate our priorities
and find meaning in small things. This time of crisis
even strengthened our marriage. Our friends and faith
community were supportive and helped us survive those
years. Our children learned to be frugal and live within
their means. We each got in touch with our expansive
spirits that continue to sustain us and help us face the
challenges in our lives.*

Leon Fleisher is a rich example of sustained spirit. For his entire life, the love of music and the opportunity to share that passion as a concert pianist was what motivated him. He has been on stage throughout the world for more than 70 years. Partway through his career, he developed problems with his right hand and learned how to play with just his left hand.

Ten years later, with treatment that restored mobility to his damaged hand, he once again became a two-handed pianist. All his former skill came back. As the featured guest of the Baltimore Symphony, he took his position on the stage at age 90 to perform with his usual skill. He walked to the piano with some unsteadiness, but when he sat on the bench, he was back in the world that gave him purpose.

Generous with our time and talents

Character is strengthened by cultivating a spirit of gratitude and generosity in good and bad times. Turning to the needs of others gives us a fresh perspective outside of ourselves. We can become as enriched as the people we serve. We can take on a new identity that may be quite different from the one we've usually had.

During these years when we are still committed to our work, many of us discover the value of mentoring. We may meet with young persons to help them with homework, music, sports, or life skills. Our mentoring helps them to build confidence in mastering or completing tasks. The effects can be long lasting.

Or we may find opportunities to mentor young adults or colleagues. Our time together may focus on their career, finances, and family life. The mentoring may be structured, or we may offer it more informally by being an example of how to live. We mentor not as experts or superiors, but as *companions*.

Generous with finances

We suggest that you develop a financial plan and update your will so your generosity is always expressed in the ways you want, reflecting your values. Maintaining a generous spirit influences who we are and sets a good example for others.

Jerry and Linda are grateful that they are able to give financially while they are still living. They see no point in waiting until they die to distribute their assets to family and various charities. They feel invested in the causes they support because they believe in their missions. One benefit in giving now is the knowledge that their gifts are supporting organizations that match their values.

From a business perspective, it is important to Jerry to choose organizations that maximize their contribution by giving directly to people in need. He and Linda support agencies such as a college they feel close to, and an economic development organization which helps small businesses in developing countries.

Linda and Jerry also have a passion to share assets with their adult children. They prefer doing it now over having their children wait for an inheritance until the time of their deaths. They find it rewarding to see how each family member is using the money responsibly, including generous giving to others.

In Jerry's and Linda's families, generosity has been modeled for several generations. Even though Linda's parents lived on a modest income, they gave 10% of what they earned to the church and to charity. Jerry also witnessed his parents' generous attitude as they shared abundantly with others. His father invited him to become a partner in his business, giving Jerry the freedom to take risks and expand the business. Jerry's father was also generous with his two daughters. What this taught Jerry was the importance of making these decisions in a timely way to preserve family harmony.

Jerry and Linda are moved emotionally as they watch persons who give sacrificially from more modest resources. They wonder if they are generous enough, even though their dollars may be in larger amounts.

They welcome this tension as a way of guiding their decisions about financial giving.

Adapting our values

What we (the authors) have experienced and witnessed in our counseling practice is that when persons focus all of their attention on their careers and getting ahead financially, they miss the opportunity to create meaningful time with family, friends, and co-workers. In other words, the choices we make now will help to determine whether our lives turn out to be what we hope for, or less than we intended.

If we want to be defined by more than our work, power, or prestige, we can make changes now that extend our sense of purpose and prepare us for a meaningful life in the days we have left. We want our loved ones and others to see us as humble, gentle, and at peace with ourselves. Even in times of challenges and loss, we can exude wisdom, compassion, and gratitude.

Spirituality

Expanding our spiritual self is at the center of this journey for many of us. A deepened faith can help us discover that the beyond is deeply embedded in the present.

Our journey is likely to find strong support through a relationship with a faith community. Such a community can provide a social support system, better self-control, and a higher sense of purpose. We (the authors) never doubted our decision to move closer to our faith community despite the financial setback because of our housing crisis. Our children benefited from a strong youth program at our church and the friends they made there. Our church-based friendships continue to support us as we navigate the changes we face as we age.

Above all, our faith creates a connection to the Source of something higher than ourselves. We are grateful for the respect, compassion, gratitude, charity, humility, harmony, meditation, and preservation of health that we have drawn from our religious tradition. Some measurements report that these values seem to forecast longevity and a sense of well-being.

We have also found it helpful to seek times of solitude. Jesus himself needed time away from others to pray and reflect. Prayer, meditation, and various forms of relaxation have been shown to decrease stress and lower one's heart rate. These practices can aid in preventing disease and improve our recovery time when we are ill. A spiritual connection gives us peace and confidence to face our challenges. It can sustain us now and into the future as we face the ends of our lives. There is no better time to make these discoveries than now.

Summary

Find a quiet few hours soon to look backward to your beginnings, size up an honest perspective of where you are at the moment, and imagine how you might start to prepare for your future. Most of us have, in the words of poet Robert Frost, "promises to keep and miles to go before we sleep." May you walk those miles thoughtfully, joyfully, and purposefully. Doing so will give you a good prospect, then, of experiencing grace and peace in retirement.

Reflecting

1. Moving from focusing on success to discovering how to live generously, while experiencing good relationships in pre-retirement, is vital to having a meaningful retirement.
2. Changing your expectation of aging from fear and loss to embracing aging as a normal part of life frees you to live more purposefully.
3. What situations in the past strengthened your resiliency?
4. How are you being generous with others?
5. What role does spirituality play in your life?

Next Steps

1. Continue to respond to the needs of others.
2. Surround yourself with positive people.
3. Give and receive love generously.
4. Re-awaken, as much as you can, the curiosity that you experienced as a child.
5. Practice breathing deeply and enjoying the moment.
6. Laugh often.

Notes

Chapter 1, Conversations About the Future, page 21, Jane E. Brody, "A Positive Outlook May Be Good for Your Health," *The New York Times*, March 27. 2017.

Chapter 5, Past as Prologue, page 77, Dr. Loren L. Johns "Historical Interest Among the Aging," *Mennonite Historical Society Newsletter*, Vol 23, 2018, p. 1.

Chapter 6, It Takes a Community, page 84, Julianne Holtz-Lunstad, "Social Relationships and Mortality Risk," *PLOS/Medicine*, July 27, 2010. Referenced in Mandy Oaklander, *Time Magazine*, February 26, 2018, p. 80.

Chapter 6, It Takes a Community, page 85, Glenn Sparks, "Forecasting Friends Forever: A longitudinal investigation of sustained closeness between best friends," *Journal of Personal Relationships*, Vol 14, #2, June, 2007, pp. 342-350.

Chapter 8, Maintaining Health, page 119, Mark Olfson, Carlos Blanco, Steven C. Marcus, "Treatment of Adult Depression in the United States," *JAMA Internal Medicine* 176 (10), 2016, pp. 1482-1491.

Chapter 9, Financial Planning, page 127, Michelle Singletary, "Pay Off That Mortgage Before Retirement," *The Washington Post*, April 16, 2018.

Chapter 10, Decisions About Housing and Possessions, page 153, Colin Holmes, "The State of American Moves: Stats and Facts," *USA Today*, April 23, 2018.

Bibliography

Christensen, Clayton M. *How Will You Measure Your Life?* New York: Harper Collins, 2012.

Creagan, M.D., Edward T. *Mayo Clinic on Healthy Aging. Rochester,* MN: Mayo Clinic, 2013.

Friedman, Howard. *The Longevity Project. New York: Gildan Media, 2011.*

Good, Merle. *Surviving Failure.* Lancaster, PA: Walnut Street Books, 2018.

Hone, Lucy. *Resilient Grieving: Finding Strength and Embracing Life after Loss that Changes Everything.* New York: The Experiment, 2017.

Jenkins, JoAnn. *Disrupt Aging.* New York: Public Affairs, 2016.

Kaufman, Gerald W. & L. Marlene Kaufman. *Necessary Conversations Between Families and their Aging Parents*, 2nd ed. New York: Good Books, 2017.

Lefever, Allon. *Launching the Entrepreneur Ship*. Centennial, CO: WordServe Literary, 2017.

Niederhaus, Sharon Graham and John L. Graham. *All in the Family: A Practical Guide for Successful Multigenerational Living.* Lanham, MD: Taylor Trade Publishers, 2013.

Parr, Carolyn Miller and Sig Cohen. *Love's Way.* Peabody, MA: Hendrickson Publishers, 2019.

Witmer, Dave. *Retirement Radicals.* Maitland, FL: Xulon Press, 2015.

Acknowledgments

We give thanks for our four adult children and their spouses, Brent and Cheryl, Nate and Cathy, Anne and Todd, and Nina and Craig, who are living the ideas covered in this book. We have included some of their stories. They are facing their present realities with intention and courage, while robustly engaging the fullness that is present in their lives. We learn from them what it is like to be in the 50s now.

Stan Shantz and Tim Jantz have been inspirational advisors as we've worked on the book. Merle and Phyllis Good of Walnut Street Books have offered guidance, support, and a commitment to marketing. Margaret High's work as our editor has been invaluable. Our sincere thanks to each of you.

About the Authors

Gerald W. Kaufman, MSW, and L. Marlene Kaufman, MSW, have each been family therapists in a joint private practice. Their specialties have been family issues, aging, and end-of-life conversations. The Kaufmans are also the authors of the book, *Necessary Conversations Between Families and Their Aging Parents.*

They have four children and eleven grandchildren. The Kaufmans live near Lancaster, Pennsylvania.